lonely planet

W9-DIV-557

Moroccan
Arabic
PHRASEBOOK & DICTIONARY

Acknowledgments
Associate Publisher Mina Patria
Managing Editor Angela Tinson
Editor Branislava Vladisavljevic
Series Designer Mark Adams
Managing Layout Designer Chris Girdler
Layout Designer Nicholas Colicchia
Language Writers Bichr Andjar, Dan Bacon, Abdennabi Benchehda

Thanks
Ruth Cosgrove, Tony Wheeler

Published by Lonely Planet Publications Pty Ltd
ABN 36 005 607 983

4th Edition – January 2014
ISBN 978 1 74179 137 2
Text © Lonely Planet 2014
Cover Image Essaouira market, Izzet Keribar/Alamy ©

Printed in China   10 9 8 7 6 5 4 3 2

Contact lonelyplanet.com/contact

MIX
Paper from
responsible sources
FSC™ C021741

acknowledgments

about the authors

Dan Bacon is an American who lived for eight years in Morocco where he started and managed Crown English Bookshop in the town of Agadir. Dan is currently employed as an engineer in the United States.

Bichr Andjar is a Moroccan who grew up and currently lives in Agadir, Morocco. He studied linguistics at the University of Agadir and has taught Moroccan Arabic to American Peace Corps Volunteers. Bichr is currently employed at the Airport in Agadir.

Many thanks to Abdennabi Benchehda for his work on the Sustainable Travel chapter.

from the authors

The authors wish to thank all of their friends in Agadir for their help in proofreading and making suggestions for the third edition of the phrasebook. Dan would like to thank his wife Kerry and sons Nate and Zach for their patience and understanding during the project.

from the publisher

Vicki Webb co-edited the book, along with Justin Rudelson who provided linguistic expertise between fending off Australian wildlife. Peter D'Onghia proofread and kept a sanguine eye on production. Brendan Dempsey designed and laid out the book with the aid of Penelope Richardson, but didn't make the cast of Falcon Crest, and Chelle Rudelson created the illustrations.

The second edition of the Lonely Planet Moroccan Arabic phrasebook was written by Dan Bacon and Bichr Andjar. Rachel Williams, with help from the LP language gurus, commissioned new content for the third edition. The French and Berber chapters were compiled at Lonely Planet.

make the most of this phrasebook ...

Anyone can speak another language! It's all about confidence. Don't worry if you can't remember your school language lessons or if you've never learnt a language before. Even if you learn the very basics (on the inside covers of this book), your travel experience will be the better for it. You have nothing to lose and everything to gain when the locals hear you making an effort.

finding things in this book

For easy navigation, this book is in sections. The Pronunciation and Grammar chapters are the ones you'll thumb through time and again. The Getting Around and Accommodation chapters cover basic travel situations like catching transport and finding a bed. The Meeting People chapter gives you conversational phrases and the ability to express opinions – so you can get to know people. Food has a section all of its own: gourmets and vegetarians are covered and local dishes feature. The Health and Emergencies chapters equip you with health and police phrases, just in case. Use the comprehensive Index to find everything easily. Otherwise, check the traveller's Dictionary for the word you need.

being understood

Throughout this book you'll see coloured phrases on each page. They're phonetic guides to help you pronounce the language. Start with them to get a feel for how the language sounds. The Pronunciation chapter will explain more, but you can be confident that if you read the coloured phrase, you'll be understood.

communication tips

Body language, ways of doing things, sense of humour – all have a role to play in every culture. The boxes included throughout this phrasebook give you useful cultural and linguistic information that will help you communicate with the locals and enrich your travel experience.

CONTENTS

INTRODUCTION

One of the first things you'll notice about Morocco is its linguistic diversity. French, Berber, Modern Standard Arabic, as well as Moroccan Arabic, can all be heard in the major cities, mainly due to the rich historical past of the country. The Berbers, the original inhabitants, make up roughly half of the population, and the three major dialects of their language are widely spoken. When the Arabs came to Morocco in the 8th century they brought their language, which has evolved into the Moroccan Arabic of today. France officially entered the picture in 1912 when it began the Moroccan protectorate and French is still widely used in commerce and the educational system.

When one speaks of Arabic in Morocco there are two languages to be considered. On the one hand there is Modern Standard Arabic. This is the direct descendant of the language of the Koran and is understood throughout the contemporary Arab world. In Morocco it's used in newspapers, correspondence, news broadcasts and speeches but rarely in conversation. Moroccan Arabic, on the other hand, is the first language of the majority of Moroccans and really the most useful language to know when travelling in the country. It differs from Modern Standard Arabic to the extent that non-Moroccan speakers of Arabic, with the possible exception of Algerians and Tunisians, find it difficult to understand.

Moroccan Arabic is strictly a spoken language and rarely written down. When it is written, the Modern Standard Arabic script is used and therefore has been adopted in this book. However, the script does reflect Moroccan Arabic pronunciation. It should prove useful to those who have had some previous exposure to Arabic as well as those wishing to make an attempt at learning the script. If you can't make yourself understood verbally, the script will be easily understood by Moroccans so you can point out the phrase you wish to communicate. Remember that Arabic script is read right to left starting from the top line.

INTRODUCTION

This phrasebook has been designed to provide the language you'll need to survive as an independent traveller in Morocco, including Moroccan Arabic and basic introductions to French and Berber. It's also an invaluable complement to the guidebook, *Morocco*, published by Lonely Planet. Enjoy yourself and good luck!

ABBREVIATIONS USED IN THIS BOOK

adj	adjective
f	female
m	male
n	noun
pl	plural
sg	singular
v	verb

PRONUNCIATION

Most of the sounds in Moroccan Arabic are similar to English and correspond to the Roman letters used to represent them here. Sounds which don't correspond as closely to the Roman letters are explained in this chapter. Several of the Arabic sounds will be new to the native English speaker and difficult at first to produce. Take comfort in the knowledge that perfect pronunciation is not necessary for you to be understood and that Moroccans are quite patient and willing to help.

VOWELS
Short Vowels
a   as the 'a' in 'at', very short
e   as the 'a' in 'about', very short
i   as the 'i' in 'hit'
u   as the 'oo' in 'book'

Long Vowels
ā   as the 'a' in 'father'
ī   as the 'ee' in 'see'
ō   as the 'oa' in boat
ū   as the 'oo' in 'boot'

Diphthongs
ai   as the 'y' in 'fly'
ow   as the 'ow' in cow
ei   as the 'ai' in 'wait'

CONSONANTS
Many Moroccan Arabic consonants are similar to those found in English, but there are some you should note. It might be useful to have a native speaker demonstrate these sounds.

g	pronounced as the 'g' in 'go', not as the 'g' in 'gentle'
gh	a guttural 'r' approximated by gargling gently. Similar to the French 'r'
H	similar to an English 'h', except pronounced deep in the throat with a loud raspy whisper. Try whispering 'hey you' loudly from as deep in the throat as possible
kh	similar to 'gh', except without the musical buzz from the voice box and similar to the 'ch' in German 'bach'
q	similar to 'k', except pronounced further back in the throat
r	trilled, as in the Spanish 'r'
zh	as the 's' in 'pleasure'
'	a glottal stop, as the sound heard between the vowels in 'uh-oh'
ᶜ	may be approximated by saying the 'a' in 'fat' with the tongue against the bottom of the mouth and from as deep in the throat as possible

Emphatic Consonants

The emphatic consonants ḍ, ṣ and ṭ are pronounced with greater muscular tension in the mouth and throat and with a raising of the back of the tongue towards the roof of the mouth. This sensation can be approximated by prolonging the 'll' sound in pull.

The letters l, r, and z can occasionally be pronounced emphatically and are indicated in the book by a double consonant. Note in particular 'God', llah

GRAMMAR

This chapter provides enough of the basics to get you communicating in Moroccan Arabic. Literal translations are provided when the word order of Arabic differs from English.

ARTICLES

In English the definite article is indicated by the word 'the'. The definite article in Moroccan Arabic is expressed in one of two ways, depending on the first sound of the following word. If the first letter is b, f, g, h, k, m, ', q, gh, h or ʿ, then l is pronounced at the beginning of the word. If the word begins with d, ḍ, n, r, s, ṣ, sh, t, ṭ, z, or zh, then the initial letter is lengthened.

When making nouns and adjectives definite, the rule to follow is – if the first letter of the word is made with the tip or front part of the tongue then it is doubled. Otherwise place an l at the beginning.

bus	kar	the bus	lkar
paper/leaf	werqa	the paper/leaf	lwerqa
place	blāṣa	the place	lblāṣa
house	ḍar	the house	ḍḍar
street	zenqa	the street	zzenqa
price	taman	the price	ttaman

One unique feature of Moroccan Arabic is that the definite article is used with adjectives as well as nouns. See Adjectives and Building Sentences on pages 19 and 27 for examples.

ROOTS & PATTERNS

The concepts of 'roots' and 'patterns' are basic in understanding how Moroccan Arabic words are formed. Most words are built on a group of letters called roots. These roots are most often made up of three letters but can be four or, less frequently, two. The root appears with various vowels and consonants which make up patterns, and usually has some fundamental meaning that's modified by the pattern.

Here are two examples. The root ktb which always has a meaning associated with writing and ⁽lm is associated with information or learning:

kteb	he wrote
mektūb	written
ktab	book
ktūb	books
mektaba	bookshop
katība	secretary
mektab	office
⁽lem	he was informed; he found out
⁽allem	he taught
t⁽allem	he learned
ta⁽līm	education
m⁽allem	master in field or profession
mu⁽allem	teacher

NOUNS

All nouns in Moroccan Arabic are either masculine or feminine. In general, nouns ending in a are feminine while those ending with any other letter are masculine.

Masculine		Feminine	
morning	sbah	food	makla
book	ktab	newspaper	zharīda
beach	bher	bed	namūsīya

Some exceptions include:

country	blad (f)	road/way	traiq (f)
hand	yedd (f)	sun	shemsh (f)
oil	zīt (f)	evening	msa (m)
ring	khatem (f)	water	lma (m)

Plural

Forming the plural of nouns in Moroccan Arabic is more complicated than in English. Each singular noun has its own plural form which is usually difficult to predict. The two most common ways of forming plurals are adding -īn to the end of masculine nouns and -at to feminine ones. There are many other patterns, so when learning words try to memorise the plural as well as the singular form.

Singular		Plural
hand	yedd	yeddīn
inspector	mūfetīsh	mūfetīshīn
bed	namūsīya	namūsīyat

PRONOUNS

Pronouns are divided into subject pronouns and object pronouns.

Subject Pronouns	
I	ana
you (m)	nta
you (f)	ntī
he/it	hūwa
she/it	hīya
we	hna
you (pl)	ntūma
they	hūma

GRAMMAR

Object Pronouns

me	-ī
you	-k
him/it	-ū
her/it	-ha
us	-na
you (pl)	-kum
them	-hum

Rather than appearing as separate words as in English, the object pronouns are attached to the end of other words in Moroccan Arabic.

he brought me	zhabī
he gave me	'ṭānī
he brought him	zhabū
he brought her	zhabha
he brought them	zhabhum

Alternative forms of the object pronouns 'me' and 'him/it' are used when the final letter preceding the pronoun is a vowel.

to, for me	liīya
to, for him/it	līh

POSSESSIVE

Possession is most often expressed by the preposition dyal- followed by the appropriate object pronoun.

That shirt is mine.	dak llqamīzha dyaī
	(lit: that the-shirt belongs-to-me)
Her room is small.	lbīt dyalha sghīra
	(lit: the-room belonging-to-her small)

The possessives of certain nouns, particularly family members, are formed by attaching an object pronoun to the end of the noun.

friend	sahbū
her friend	sahbha
our friend	sahbna

Note that when the noun is feminine, the final a of the feminine noun changes to at:

mother	walīda
my mother	walīdatī
their mother	walīdathum

ADJECTIVES

Adjectives follow nouns in the sentence and must agree in gender and number. That is, if a noun is feminine and singular then the adjective that follows it must be feminine and singular as well.

Feminine and plural forms of adjectives are derived from the masculine base form. The feminine form of the adjective is formed simply by adding -a. The plural form of adjectives, as with nouns, is difficult to predict. The two most common patterns are adding -īn ('pretty', zwīn – zwīnīn) or replacing the long vowel sound in the middle of the word with a ('big', kbīr – kbar).

GRAMMAR

the small bed	nnamūsīya ṣṣghīra
	(lit: the-bed the-small)
the small beds	nnamūsīyat ssghar
	(lit: the-beds the-smalls)
He is big.	hūwa kbīr
She is tall.	hiya kbīra
They are tall.	hūma kbar

Comparative

The most common way of forming comparatives is to remove the long vowel from the regular adjective form (eg 'big' -kbīr, 'bigger'-kber).

| He is bigger than my son. | hūwa kber men weldī |
| | (lit: he bigger than son-my) |

VERBS

The following is an example of the way the present, past and future tenses are formed for the verb ktb , 'to write', in which all three letters of the root are consonants. Roots in which the middle or final letter is a vowel will differ slightly, but this should give a general idea of how the verb structure works. It isn't necessary to say the pronoun (I, we, you, etc) with the verb as it is in English. Every pronoun has a particular verb form, so it's clear from the verb alone who is performing the action.

ktb – 'to write'

Present Tense

I write, am writing	kan(kt)e(b)
you (m) write, are writing	kat(kt)e(b)
you (f) write, are writing	kat(k)e(tb)ī
he/it writes, is writing	kay(kt)e(b)
she/it writes, is writing	kat(kt)e(b)
we write, are writing	kan(k)e(tb)ū
you (pl) write, are writing	kat(k)e(tb)ū
they write, are writing	kay(k)e(tb)ū

Past Tense

I wrote	(kt)e(b)t
you wrote	(kt)e(b)tī
he/it wrote	(kt)e(b)
she/it wrote	(k)e(tb)at
we wrote	(kt)e(b)na
you (pl) wrote	(kt)e(b)tū
they wrote	(k)e(tb)ū

Future Tense

I will write	ghadī n(kt)e(b)
you (m) will write	ghadī t(kt)e(b)
you (f) will write	ghadī t(k)e(tb)ī
he/it will write	ghadī ī(kt)e(b)
she/it will write	ghadī t(kt)e(b)
we will write	ghadī n(k)e(tb)ū
you (pl) will write	ghadī t(k)e(tb)ū
they will write	ghadī ī(k)e(tb)ū

GRAMMAR

TO BE
Present tense

A verb usually isn't required when expressing 'to be' in the present tense, unless a re-occurring action is being described.

She's sick.	hīya mreiḍa (lit: she sick)
We are in Marrakesh.	hena felmerraksh (lit: we-are in-Marrakesh)
He's at the hospital on Mondays.	hūwa keikūn fessebīṭār nnhar letnīn (lit: he is at-the-hospital day on Mondays)

kan – 'to be'	
I am	kankūn
you are	katkūn
he/it is	keikun
she/it is	katkuun
we are	kankūnū
you are (pl)	katūnū
they are	keikūnū

Expressing 'to be' in the past tense is similar to English except that it isn't necessary to use a pronoun.

Past Tense	
I was	kunt
you were	kuntī
he/it was	kan
she/it was	kant
we were	kunna
you were (pl)	kuntū
they were	kanū

GRAMMAR

I was sick yesterday.	kunt mrīd lbareh
	(lit: I-was sick yesterday)
We were in Marrakesh last week.	kunna felmerraksh l'ūsbū' llī fat
	(lit: we-were in-Marrakesh the-week that-passed)

Future Tense

I will be	ghādī nkūn
you will be	ghādī tkūn
he/it will be	ghādī īkūn
she/it will be	ghādī tkūn
we will be	ghādī nkūnū
you (pl) will be	ghādī tkūnū
they will be	ghādī īkūnū

| We are going to be in Marrakesh tomorrow. | hena ghādī nkūnu felmerraksh ghedda |

There is/There are

kein (m)/keina (f)/keinīn (pl) are a special form of the verb 'to be', used to express 'there is/there are' in Moroccan Arabic. It's most commonly used with nouns, and agrees with the noun in gender and number.

There's a doctor in Marrakesh.	kein ṭṭōbeb felmerraksh
There are tomatoes at the *souq*.	lmaṭeisha keinīn fessūq
It's raining.	keina shshta
	(lit: there is rain)

GRAMMAR

KEY VERBS

to arrive	wsel
to be	kan
to bring	zhab
to come	zha
to cost	swa
to depart	ghrezh
to do	dar
to go	msha
to have	*See below*
to know	ʿref
to live	ʿash
to make	dar
to meet	tlaqa
to need	htazh
to pay	ghelleş
to prefer	fḍel
to return	rzha
to say	gal
to stay	bqa
to take	ghad
to talk	tklem
to understand	fhem
to walk	temsha

GRAMMAR

TO HAVE

'To have' is expressed in Moroccan Arabic by the preposition ʿand, literally 'in the possession of', followed by an object pronoun.

I have	ʿandī
you have	ʿandek
he/it has	ʿandū
she/it has	ʿandha

we have	ʿandna
you have (pl)	ʿandkum
they have	ʿandhum

I have the ticket.	ʿandī lwurqa
They have the ticket.	ʿandhōm lwurqa
Do you have the ticket?	ʿandek lwurqa?

Expressing 'to have' in the past tense may seem confusing initially. It's accomplished by preceding ʿand with the form of kan (see 'to be' past tense on page 20). ʿand must match the subject of the sentence in gender and number and kan must match the object in gender and number.

I had the ticket.	kanet ʿandī lwurqa
I had the tickets.	kanū ʿandī lwūraq
He had the ticket.	kanet ʿandū lwurqa
He had the tickets.	kanū ʿandū lwūraq

MODALS
These are formed by placing two verbs next to each other in the sentence.

To Want
I want to go	bghīt nemshī
you want to go	bghītī temshī
he wants to go	bgha yemshī
she wants to go	bghat temshī

we want to go	bghīna nemshīw
you (pl) want to go	bghītū temshīw
they want to go	bghaw yemshīw

To Need
I need to go	khessnī nemshī
you need to go	khessek temshī
he needs to go	khessū yemshī
she needs to go	khessha temshī

GRAMMAR

we need to go	khessna nemshīw
you (pl) need to go	khesskum temshīw
they need to go	khesshum yemshīw

QUESTIONS

A statement can be made into a question by either changing your voice inflection, as in English, or by preceding the statement with wash.

This wallet is mine.	had lbeztām dyalī
	(lit: this the-wallet belonging-to-me)
Is this wallet mine?	wash had lbeztām dyalī?
	(lit: does this the-wallet belong-to-me)

Question Words

who	shkūn
what	ash
when	īmta
where	fīn
why	ⁿlash
how	kīfash
whose	dyalmen
which	ashmen
how much	shhal

What's that?	ash dak shī?
	(lit: what that stuff)
When will it come?	īmta ghadī izhī?
	(lit: when going it-come)
Where's the bank?	fīn lbānka?
	(lit: where the-bank)
How much is it?	shhal kayswa?
	(lit: how-much it-costs)

GRAMMAR

NEGATIVES

A sentence can be made negative by placing ma- at the beginning of the verb and -sh at the end of it.

He came on time.	zha felweqt
	(lit: he-came on-the-time)
He didn't come on time.	mazhash felweqt
	(lit: not-he-came on-the-time)

A sentence without a verb can be made negative by using mashī with an adjective.

The price is cheap.	ttaman rkhais
	(lit: the-price cheap)
The price is not cheap.	ttamam mashī rkhais
	(lit: the-price not cheap)

PREPOSITIONS

These prepositions don't occur separately but are fixed to the beginning of other words (eg 'the house' ddar, 'in the house' feddar).

with; by; by means of	b-/bī-
from; than	men-
between	bīn-/bīnat-
with	mʿa-
without	bla-
before	qbel-
in front of; facing	gôddam-
after	beʿd-
under; below	teht-
of; belonging to	d-/dyal-
behind	wra-
in; among	f-/fī-
on	ʿla-/ʿlī-
over; above	fuq-
next to	hda-
to; for	l-/lī-

GRAMMAR

CONJUNCTIONS

Conjunctions link things in a sentence. These things could be nouns, phrases or clauses.

or	awla
when/since	mnīn
in order to	bash
and	wô
if	īla/kūn
but	walakīn
until	hetta
even though	wakhkha
since	mellī

THIS & THAT

this	had
that (f)	dīk
that (m)	dak
those	dūk
this one (m)	hada
that one (m)	hadak
this one (f)	hadi
that one (f)	hadīk
these ones	hadū
those ones	hadūk
this thing/situation	had shī
that thing/situation	dak shī

GRAMMAR

this book	had lektab
	(lit: this the-book)
that girl	dīk lbent
	(lit: that the-girl)
That (one) is very good.	mezyan bezzaf hadak
	(lit: good very that one)

BUILDING YOUR OWN SENTENCES

As mentioned on page 20, the equivalent of the English verb 'to be' isn't normally required in Moroccan Arabic when speaking in the present tense. In this type of sentence the subject usually comes first.

I'm a teacher.	ana ᶜusted
	(lit: I teacher)
That man is at the hotel.	dak rrazhel felūtail
	(lit: that the-man at-the-hotel)

A simple sentence can be formed using a noun with the definite article followed by an adjective without the definite article.

The view is beautiful.	lmender zwīn
	(lit: the-view beautiful)
The bed is small.	nnamūsīya sghīra
	(lit: the-bed small)

GRAMMAR

Where a verb is present, the subject of a sentence can be placed either before or after the verb. Subject pronouns don't need to be stated as the subject can be understood by the form of the verb.

I went to the restaurant.	mshīt llmet'am
	(lit: I-went to-the-restaurant)
The train left.	kherzhat lmashīna
	(lit: left the-train)

GRAMMAR

MEETING PEOPLE

Moroccans are legendary for their friendliness and hospitality. Most of them will be thrilled at your attempt to use their language and you'll have no trouble striking up conversations.

YOU SHOULD KNOW

Yes.	īyeh	ايه
No.	la	لا
OK.	wakha	وخة
Please.	ʿafak	عفاك
Thank you.	shukran	شكرا
	barak llāhū fīk	بارك الله في

Thank you very much.
  shukran bezzef
شكرا بزاف
Without honour. (response to thank you)
  bla zhmīl
بلا جميل
You're welcome.
(lit: You don't need to thank me for my duty.)
  la shukran ʿla wezhb
لا شكرا علي واجب
Excuse me.
  smeh līya
اسمح لي
No problem. (response to excuse me)
  makein mūshkīl
ماكاين مشكل

GREETINGS & GOODBYES

When greeting Moroccans you'll find them more expressive than you might be accustomed to. One example of this is their liberal use of handshakes. Remember it's polite to shake each person's hand when entering a room or encountering a group of people. If this becomes unrealistic, pronouncing the phrase ssalamū ʿlekum is an acceptable substitute. Also notice that a handshake should be followed by placing your hand over your heart. It's common to greet close friends of the same sex by kissing them on both cheeks, especially if you haven't seen them recently.

The following phrases can be used when approaching someone you don't know. The first, ssalamū ˤlekum , is universal throughout the Arab world and appropriate for greeting both one person and groups.

Peace be upon you.	ssalamū ˤlekum	السلام عليكم
Good morning.	ṣbah lkhīr	صباح الخير
Good afternoon/evening.	mselkhīr	مساء الخير

The following phrases are less formal. They are spoken quickly, stringing several expressions together without necessarily waiting for a response.

How are you? (lit: No harm?)	labas?	لا باءس
How are you?	kīf halek?	كيف حالك؟
Fine, thank you.	labas, barak llāhū fīk	لا باءس بارك الله فيك
Is everything OK?	kulshi bekhīr?	كل شيء بخير؟
Fine, praise God.	bekhīr lhamdū llāh	بخير الحمد لله
What's happening?	'ash khbarek?	اش خبارك؟
How are you doing?	kī deir? (m)	كي داير؟
	kī deira? (f)	كي دايرة؟
	kī deirīn? (pl)	كي دايرين؟
Is your health OK?	ṣsehha labas?	الصحة لا باءس؟
Is your family OK?	lˤa'īla labas?	العائلة لا باءس؟
Are your children OK?	ddrarī labas?	الدراري لا باءس؟

MEETING PEOPLE

The most common way to say goodbye is bessalama. Some other expressions to use when parting company are:

Goodbye. (lit: with peace)
mᶜa ssalama
مع السلامة

Goodbye. (lit: may God give you tranquility)
lla yhennīk
الله يهنيك

May God help you. (to someone going to work)
lla yᶜuwn
الله يعون

Good night. (lit: may God grant you a good evening)
lla yemsek ᶜla khīr
الله يمسك علي خير

Take care of yourself.
thella frāṣek
تهلاً فراسك

CIVILITIES

Unlike English speakers who tend to improvise when polite remarks are expected, Moroccans draw from a large number of fixed expressions. The following are a few of the more common ones, along with the contexts in which they're used. Though not essential, these sayings will be appreciated when used correctly.

ensha'llāh
انشاء الله
    If God wills.
    (talking about the future or making plans)

tbarka llāh ᶜlīk
تبارك الله عليك
    The blessing of God upon you.
    (complimenting someone on an accomplishment)

lla ybarek fīk
الله يبارك فيك
    May God bless you.
    (response to tbarka llāh ᶜlīk)

lla ykhlef	الله يخلف
May God return it to you.	
(after receiving hospitality or getting paid)	
beṣṣāḥḥtek	بصحتك
To your health.	
(to someone after a haircut or bath)	
lla yᶜṭeik sehha	الله يعطيك الصحة
May God give you health.	
(response to beṣṣeḥhtek)	
lla ysehhel	الله يسهل
May God make it easy for you.	
(to a beggar when not giving anything)	
lla yrhem waldīk	الله يرحم والدك
May God have mercy on your parents.	
(when asking or thanking someone for help)	
ᶜla slamtek	على سلامتك
Peace upon you.	
(to someone arriving from a journey or	
recovering from an illness or calamity)	
lla ysellemek	الله يسلمك
May God grant you peace.	
(response to ᶜla slamtek)	
ṭṭreq ssalama	طريق السلامة
Have a peaceful trip.	
(to someone leaving on a journey)	
besmellāh	بسم الله
In the name of God.	
(before eating, travelling or any activity	
you wish to do in God's name)	
mbrūk!	مبروك!
Congratulations!	
mrehba bīk ᶜandna (sg)	مرحب بيك عندنا
mrehba bīkum ᶜandna (pl)	مرحب بكم عندنا
You are welcome at our house.	
(said to someone as they arrive to visit your home)	

MEETING PEOPLE

FORMS OF ADDRESS

When addressing men, asīdī 'sir', is a polite title and one appropriate to use with men in official positions. When used before a name it is shortened to sī (eg sī hamed). A common expression used to attract someone's attention on the street or when calling for the waiter in a cafe is shrīf The expression sī muhamed can also be used in this way though it's not as polite. The frequently heard title hazh (m)/ hazha (f) is ascribed to those who've made the Muslim pilgrimage to Mecca.

Alalla, equivalent to 'madam', can be used when getting the attention of a woman or when addressing her in conversation.

FIRST ENCOUNTERS

What's your name?
   asmītek?   اسميتك؟

My name is ...
   smīti ...   ... سميتى

His name is ...
   smītū ...   ... سميتو

Her name is ...
   smīthā ...   ... سميتة

I'm honoured to meet you.
   metsherrfīn   متشرفين

I'd like to introduce you to ...
   bghīt nqeddemlek ...   ... بغيت نقدم لك

MAKING CONVERSATION

Do you live here?
   wesh katskūn henna?   واش كتسكن هنا؟

Where do you live?
   fīn katskūn?   فين كتسكون؟

What are you doing?
   'ash katdīr?   اش كتدير؟

How long have you been here?
   shehal mad wenta hna?   شحل مد وانت هنا؟

MEETING PEOPLE

I've been here for ...
  mad ... wana hna
مد ... وانا هنا

I'm going to stay for ...
  ghadu nkless ...
غادو نكلس ...

This is my first visit to Morocco.
  hada marra lūla lūzhīt da lmaghreb
هد مرة لولة لوجيت د المغرب

Someone's waiting for me.
  ktesstanna lī shi wahed
كيتستنا ني شي واحد

I've had a nice day.
  hada lnhar kнabatnu
هد النهار كحباتنو

I'll call you on the phone.
  ghadī nᶜaytlīk ltelefun
غادي نعيطليك التليفون

I'm staying at ...
  ana zhaless f ...
انا جالس ف ...

I hope to see you again
  knetsefa shūfak ᶜud tānī
كنتصفا شوفك عود تاني

Where are you going?
  fein ghādī?
فين غادي؟

Useful Phrases

Where are you going?	fīn ghāde?	فين غادي؟
Watch out!	ᶜandak!	عنداك!
	balek!	بالك!
Be careful.	redd balek	ردّ بالك
It's clear/understood.	ṣāfī	صافي
Look!	shūf!	شوف!
Listen!	smaᶜ!	سمع!
Not yet.	mazel bāqī	مازال باقي
Hurry up!	serbī!	سربي!
Slow down!	beshwīya ᶜlīk!	ب شوية عليك!
I'm ready.	ana mūzhūd (m)	انا موجود
	ana mūzhūda (f)	انا موجودة
Go away!	sīr fhalek!	سير في حالك!
Leave me alone.	ᶜṭeinī ttīsaᶜ	عطيني التيساع
Leave us alone.	ᶜṭeina ttīsaᶜ	عطينا التيساع

I'll return in a little while.
ghadu nerzhaʿ men daba madl shwey · غادو نرجع من دابا ل ماد ل شوي

What do you think about ...?
'ash katfker fe ...? · اش كتفكر ف ...؟

Is it OK if I take a photo of you?
wakhkha ntṣōwwerek? · وخّا نتصورك؟

What do you call this?
'ash katsmīw hada (m)/hadī (f)? · اش كتسميو هدّ/هدي؟

This is beautiful.
zwīn hada (m)/ zwīna hadī (f) · زوين هدّ/ زوينة هدِ

We like Morocco!
ʿazhebatna lmaghrīb! · عجباتنا المغريب!

That's amazing!
ʿazhība! · عجيبة!

I'm here on ... · zhīt l lmaghrīb fe ... · جيت ل المغريب ف ...
business · felkhedma · فل الخدمة
holiday · fel ʿōṭla · فل عوطلة

Useful Phrases

Get away from me.	baʿd mennī	بعد مني
What's the matter with you?	malek?	مالك؟
That doesn't interest me.	dakshī mayhemmnīsh	داك شي ميهمنيش
Yes I can.	īyeh nqder	ايه نقدر
No I can't.	la maqdersh	لا مقدرش
It's possible.	yemken	يمكن
It isn't possible.	mayemkensh	ما يمكنش
I forgot.	nset	نسيت
too much/a lot	bezzaf	بزّاف
a little	shwiya	شوية
important	mūhim	مهم
not important	mashi mūhīm	ماشي مهم
very important	mūhīm bezzaf	مهم بزاف

MEETING PEOPLE

NATIONALITIES

Where are you from?	mnīn nta? (m)	منين انت؟
	mnīn nti? (f)	منين انت؟
	mnīn ntūma? (pl)	منين انتم؟
I'm from ...	ana men ...	انا من ...
I live in ...	ana saken fe ...	انا ساكن في ...
America	'amrīka	امريكا
Australia	ustralya	استراليا
Canada	kanada	كندا
England	anglatīra	انجلترا
France	fransa	فرنسا
Germany	almānya	المانيا
Italy	'īṭālīya	ايطاليا
Japan	el zhaban	اليابان
Morocco	lmaghrīb	المغرب
Netherlands	hulanda	هولاندا
Spain	īsbanya	اسبانيا
Sweden	sswīd	السويد
Switzerland	swīsra	سويسرا
the city	lmadīna	المدينة
the countryside	lbadīya	البادية
the mountains	lzhbel	الجبال
the suburbs of ...	ᶜla berra men ...	علي البرا من ...
I'm ...	ana ...	انا ...
American	mīrīkanī (m)	مريكاني
	mīrīkanīya (f)	مريكانية
Australian	ustralī (m)	استرالي
	ustralīya (f)	استرالية
British	neglīzī (m)	نجليزي
	neglīzīya (f)	نجليزية
French	fransawī (m)	فرنساوي
	fransawīya (f)	فرنساوية
Italian	'īṭālī (m)	ايطالي
	'īṭālīya (f)	ايطالية

Japanese	lzhabanī (m)	ياباني
	lzhabanīya (f)	يابانية
Moroccan	maghrībī (m)	مغربي
	maghrībīya (f)	مغربية
Spanish	īsbanī (m)	اسباني
	īsbanīya (f)	اسبانية
Sweden	swīdī (m)	سويدي
	swīdīya (f)	سويدية
Swiss	swīsrī (m)	سويسري
	swīsrīya (f)	سويسرية

CULTURAL DIFFERENCES

How do you do this in your country?
kīfesh katdīrū hadshī
felbladkum?

كيفاش كتديرو هد شي فل
بلادكم؟

Is this a local custom?
wesh hadshī ʿadī felbladkum?

واش هد شي عادي فل بلادكو؟

This isn't the custom in my country.
hadshee mashī ʿadī felbladna

هد شي ما شي عادي فل بلادنا

I'm not accustomed to this.
ana mamwlafsh be hadsī

انا مامولفش ب هد شي

I'd like to watch but I don't want to join in.
bghiṭ nteferrezh walakīm
mabghītsh ndekhul feha

بغيت نتفرج والاكن ما
بغيتش ندخل فيها

AGE

How old are you?	shhal f'merek?	شحال ف عمرك؟
I'm ...	'andī ...	عندي ...
18 years old	tmenṭāshal 'am	تمنطاشل عام
25 years old	khamsa ū'shrīn 'am	خمسة و عشرين عام

Note: See the Numbers chapter for your particular age.

OCCUPATIONS

What's your occupation?
ash kat'amel? (m)   اش كتعمل ؟
ash kat'amlī? (f)   اش كتعملي ؟

I'm a(n) ...	ana ...	انا ...
businessperson	tazher (m)	تاجر
	tazhra (f)	تاجرة
carpenter	nazhzhar (m)	نجار
doctor	ṭbīb (m)	طبيب
	ṭbība (f)	طبيبة
engineer/architect	mūhendīs (m)	مهندس
	mūhendīsa (f)	مهندسة
government employee	mweḍḍef (m)	موظف
	mweḍḍefa (f)	موظفة
journalist	ṣāhāfī (m)	صحافي
	ṣāhāfīya (f)	صحافية
lawyer	mūhamī (m)	محامي
	mūhamīya (f)	محامية

MEETING PEOPLE

retiree	qebt lantrīt (m/f)	قبطت لا نتريت
secretary	katīb (m)	كاتب
	katība (f)	كاتبة
student	ṭāleb (m)	طالب
	ṭāleba (f)	طالبة
teacher	'ūstad (m)	استاذ
	'ūstada (f)	استاذة

What are you studying?	ash katqrā?	اش كتنقرأ؟
I'm studying ...	kanqrā ...	كنقرأ ...
art	fenn	الفن
business	ltezhara	التجارة
education	ltalīm	التعليم
engineering	handassa	هندسة
linguistics	lghāt	لغات
law	lнkūk	الحقوق
literature	lᶜadāb	الاداب
medicine	ltebb	الطب
science	lᶜūlūm	العولوم
math	lhessāb	الحساب
chemistry	kemyāᶜ	كمياء
sociology	ᶜūlūm ezhtemāᶜya	علوم اجتماعية

MEETING PEOPLE

RELIGION

What's your religion?
  ashnū hūwa ddīn dyalek?   اشنو هو دين ديالك؟

I'm ...	ana ...	انا ...
Buddhist	būdī (m)	بودي
	būdīya (f)	بودية
Christian	masīhī (m)	مسيحي
	masīhīya (f)	مسيحية
Hindu	hendī (m)	هندي
	hendīya (f)	هندية
Jewish	īhūdī (m)	اهودي
	īhūdīya (f)	اهودية
Muslim	meslem (m)	مسلم
	meslema (f)	مسلمة

FEELINGS

I'm ...	ana ...	انا ...
bored	meqnuṭ (m)	مقنوط
	meqnuṭā (f)	مقنوطة
happy	ferhan (m)	فرحان
	ferhana (f)	فرحانة
scared	kheif (m)	خايف
	kheifa (f)	خايفة
sick	mrīḍ (m)	مريض
	mrīḍā (f)	مريضة
tired	ʿeyyan (m)	عيان
	ʿeyyana (f)	عيانة
upset/angry	mqelleq (m)	مقلق
	mqellqa (f)	مقلقة
in a hurry	zerban (m)	زربان
	zerbana (f)	زربانة
worried	mqelleq (m)	مقلق
	mqelleqa (f)	مقلقة
sad	mqelleq (m)	مقلق
	mqelleqa (f)	مقلقة

I'm hungry.	fīya zhūwaʿ	فيّ جوعة
I'm thirsty.	fīya lʿaṭesh	في العطش
I'm right.	ʿandī lhuqq	عندي الحق
I'm wrong.	mʿandīsh lhuqq	ما عنديش الحق

LANGUAGE DIFFICULTIES

I don't speak Arabic.
makanʿrefsh lʿarbīya
ما كنعرفش العربية

I only know a little Arabic.
kanʿref ghīr shī shwīya
dyal lʿarbīya
كنعرف غير شي شوية
ديال العربية

Do you speak English?
wash katʿref neglīzīya?
واش كتعرف نجليزية؟

Does anyone here speak English?
wash kein shī hedd henna
lī keiʿref neglīzīya?
واش كاين شي حدّ هنا لي
كيعرف نجليزية؟

I understand.
fhemt
فهمت

I don't understand.
mafhemtsh
ما فهمتش

Do you understand?
wash fhemtī?
واش فهمتي؟

What did you say?
ash gulltī?
اش كلتي؟

How do you say ... in Arabic?
kīfash katgūlū ... belʿarabīya?
كيفاش كتكولو . . . ب العربية؟

What does this mean?
    ash kat'anī hadhī?

اش كتعني هادي؟

Please speak slowly!
    tkellem beshwīya 'afak!

تكلم بشوية عفاك!

Translate this word for me please.
    terzhemlī had lkalma 'afak

ترجم لي هاد الكلمة عفاك

Write it down for me.
    ktebha līya

كتيبها لي

Please repeat it.
    'awwedha 'afak

عودها عفاك

Public transportation in Morocco is both inexpensive and easy to use. Within city limits, one can take either city buses or small (petit) taxis.

For trips between major cities, trains are the quickest and most comfortable means of travel, though they can be crowded at certain times of the year. The other options are buses and large (grand) taxis. The buses are the cheapest choice but can vary quite a bit in both speed and comfort. With grand taxis it is possible to pay on a per-seat basis as well as for the whole taxi.

FINDING YOUR WAY

I'm looking for ...
kanqelleb 'la ...
كنقلت علي . . .

How do I get to ...?
kīfesh ghādī nuwṣul l ...?
كفاش غادي نوصل ل . . . ؟

Is it near/far?
wash qrīb/b'ad?
واش قريب /بعيد؟

Please show me on the map.
werri liya men l kharita 'afak
وريني لي من الخريطة عفاك

Is there another way?
wesh kein shī trīq akhur?
واش كاين شي طريق اخر؟

Which way is best?
ashmen trīq hessen
اش من طريق حسن؟

Can we walk from here?
wash yemkin nzidu 'la razhelīna?
واش يمكن نزيدو علي رجلينا؟

Where is the ...?	fīn kein ...?	فين كاين . . . ؟
city bus station	mheṭṭa dyal ṭṭōbīsat	المحطة ديال ال طوبسات
intercity bus station	mheṭṭa dyal lkīran	المحطة ديال الكيران
train station	lagār	لاكار
airport	lmāṭār	المطار
taxi stand	blāṣa dyal ṭṭaksīyat	البلاصة ديال التكسيات

GETTING AROUND

Which ... is this?	ashmen ... hadī	اش من ... هد؟
city	medīna	مدينة
street	zenqa	زنقة
boulevard	sharī<	شارع

What time does the ... arrive/leave?

wufūqash keiwṣul/keikhrezh ...? (m)	وفكاش كيوصل / كيخرج ... ؟
wufūqash katwṣul/wkatkhrezh ...? (f)	وفكاش كتوصل / كتخرجي ... ؟
bus (city)	ṭṭubīs	الطوبيس
bus (intercity)	lkar	الكار
train	tran	تران
taxi	ṭṭāksī	الطاكسي
plane	ṭṭeiyyāra	الطيارة

DIRECTIONS

Go straight ahead!	sīr nīshan!	سير نيشان!
Turn right!	ḍōr <al līmen!	دور علي ليمن!
Turn left!	ḍōr <al līser!	دور علي ليسرا!

Turn at the ...	ḍōr ...	دور ...
corner	felqent	ف القنت
traffic light	feḍō elhmer	ف ضو الاحمر
roundabout	ferrumpwan	ف الرمبوان
first street	fezzenqa llewla	ف الزنقة اللولة
second street	fezzenqa tteneya	ف الزنقة التانية

after	men b<d	من بعد
avenue	sharīya	شارع
behind	men lur	من اللور

between	ma bīn	مابين
corner	qent	قنت
far	bᶜeid	بعيد
in front of/opposite	quddem	قدام
near	qrīb	قريب
next to	hedda	حدا
slow down	beshwīya ᶜlīk	بشويا عليك
square	blāṣā	بلازا
stop light	ḍu lhmer	الضو الاحمر
stop sign	stup	ستب
street	zenqa	زنقة

Go backwards!
  rzhaᶜ lur!   رجع لورا!

Cross the street!
  qtaᶜ ṭṭreq!   قطع طريق!

Continue on a little further!
  zīd qeddem wahed shwīya!   زيد قدام واحد شويا!

How far?   bshhal bᶜeid?   بشحال بعيد؟

north	shamel	الشمال
south	zhanūb	الجنوب
east	sherq	الشرق
west	gherb	الغرب

ADDRESSES

Moroccan addresses may be written in either French or classical Arabic. Written Arabic addresses usually take this format:

25 Mohammed V Boulevard
Rabat
25 shariᶜ muhamed lkhamīs   ٢٥ شارع محمد الخامس
rbāt   الرباط

GETTING AROUND

BUYING TICKETS

I'd like a ... ticket to Casablanca please.	'afak bghīt wahed lwarka l ddar lbeiḍa ...	عفاك بغيت واحد الورقة ل لدار البيضة ...
return	bash nemshī ū nzhī	نمشي و نجي
1st class	ddarazha llūla	الدرجة الأول
2nd class	ddarazha ttanīya	الدرجة الثانية

What's the fare?
shhal taman lwarka
شحال التمن ل ورقة؟

AIR

Air fares in Morocco are controlled by the national airline, Royal Air Maroc. It is the only company that offers internal flights and, while quite reasonable by international standards, is expensive compared to other forms of transportation. If you need to be somewhere in a hurry, air travel is worth checking out.

When is there a flight to ...?
'emta ghādī tkūn shī ṭeiyārāl ...?
امتي غادي تكون شي طيارة ...؟
What time do I need to be at the airport?
'ashmen sa'a kheṣṣnī nkūn felmaṭār?
اش من ساعة خصني نكون ف المطار؟
Is it a direct flight?
wash rrihla direct?
واش الرحلة دريكت؟
How long is the flight?
sh hal dyal lwaqt ta ddir ltayara?
شحال ديال الوقت تدير الطيارة؟
Is the flight full?
wash ttiyarā 'amra?
واش طيارة عامرة؟

domestic	mhalli	محلي
international	duwalli	دولي
arriving flights	lwusul	الوصول
departing flights	ddahab	الذهاب

GETTING AROUND

I'd like to ... my reservation.	bghit ... hazhz dyali	بغيت ... حجزديالي
change	bdel	بدل
confirm	eked	آا كد
cancel	lghi	الغي

What's the charge for extra luggage?
shhal khes itkhelles ala lbagazh lli zayed?

شحال خص اتخلص علي البكاج لي زايد؟

Is there a bus to the airport?
wash kain shi tubis lmatar?

واش كاين شي طوبيس للمطار؟

Where can I catch a taxi to the airport?
fin khesni mshed taxi Lmatar?

فين خصني مشد طاكسي ل مطار؟

I'd like to check in my luggage.
bghit nszhzhel l bagazh dyali

بغيت نسجل البكاج ديالي

What's the flight number?
shhal rraqem dyal rrihla?

شحال الرقم ديال الرحلة؟

My luggage hasn't arrived.
llbagazh dyali ma weselsh

البكاج ديالي ما وصلش

BUS

local bus	ṭōbus	طوبيس
intercity bus	lkar	الكار

Give me two tickets to ... please.
qettaⁿli zhūzh dyal lwraq l ... ʿafak

قطع لي جوج ديال الوُراق ل ... عفاك

What time does the first/last bus leave?
wuqtash kaykhrezh lkar lewwel/lakher?

وقتاش كيخرج الكاراللول / الاخر؟

GETTING AROUND

Where's this bus going?

fīn ghādī had lkar?   فين غادي هد الكار؟

Is this bus going to ...?

wash had lkar ghādī l ...?   واش هد الكار غادي ل ... ؟

How much is it for a ticket from here to ...?

shhal kat^cmel lwerqa bash   شحال كتعمل الورقة
nemshī men henna l ...?   باش نمشي من هنا ل ... ؟

Which bus is going to ...?

ashmen kar ghādī l ...?   أش من كار غادي ل ... ؟

Where can I catch a bus to ...?

fīn yemkenlī nqbed lkar l ...?   فين يمكن لي نكبد الكار ل ... ؟

When's the bus going to come?

'īmta ghādī īzhī lkar?   امتي غادي ياجي الكار؟

How many buses per day go to ...?

shhal men kar kaymshī l   شحال من كار كيمشي ل ... ف
... fenhar?   نهار؟

Is ... far from here?

wash ... b^ceid men henna?   واش ... بعيد من هنا؟

Is ... near here?

wash ... qrīb l henna?   واش ... قريب لهنا؟

Please tell me when we arrive at ...

^cafak īla wṣelna l ... gūlhalīya   عفاك الي وصلنا ل ... كولهالي

Let me off here.

ōnzzelni henna   نزلني هنا

TRAIN

Where's the train station?
  fīn kein lagār?
فين كاين لاكار؟

Is this train going to ...?
  wash had ltran ghādi l ...?
واش هاد تران غادي ل . . . ؟

Please give me two 1st/2nd class tickets.
  ʿafak qeṭṭaʿli zhūzh lweraq dyal
  dārāzha lewwla/tanīya
عفاك قطع لي جوج وراق ديال
الدرجة الولي / الثانية

Is this seat free?
  wash had lblāṣā khawīya?
واش هد البلاصة خاوية؟

This seat is taken.
  had lblāṣāʿamra
هد البلاصة عامرة

Would you mind if I opened the window?
  wash makein mūshkīl īla hlīt
  sserzhem?
واش مكين مشكل الا هليت
سرزهم؟

Where do I need to change trains?
  fīn kheṣṣnī nbeddel tran?
فين خصني نبدل تران؟

TAXI

Is there a taxi stand near here?
  wash kein shī blāṣādyal
  ṭṭaksīat qrība l henna?
واش كاين شي بلاصة ديال
الطاكسيات قريبة من هنا؟

How much for us to go to ...?
  shhal khesna knkkhlṣu hash
  nemshiiw?
شحال خصنا نخلصو
باش نمشون ل . . . ؟

I want to pay for one place only.
  bghīt nkhelleṣ blāṣāwaheda
بغيت نخلص بلاصة وحدة

I want to travel with other people
  bghīt nesafer mʿa nas khrin
بغيت نسافر مع ناس خرين

Do we need to pay extra for luggage?
  wash khesna nekhlṣu shi ziyada
  ala lbagazh?
واش خصنا نخلصو شي زيادة
علي البكاج؟

Do you have change?
  wash endak elserf ?
واش عندك الصرف؟

Go slowly please.
  temsha bshwīya ʿafak
تمشي بشوي عفاك

Stop here please.
wqef henna 'afak
وقف هنا عفاك

I'd like to get out here please.
bghīt nenzel henna 'afak
بغيت ننزل هنا عفاك

Take me to ...	wesselnī l ...	... وصلني ل
this address	had l'unwen	هدا العنوان
the airport	lmāṭār	المطار
the bank	lbānka	البنكة

I'm in a hurry.
ana zerban (m)   انا زربان
ana zerbana (f)   انا زربانة

Please wait for me.
tsennanī 'afak   تسناني عفاك

I'll be right back.
daba nzhī   داب نجي

Stop!
'ūqef!   وقف!

CAR

Where can I rent a car?
fin yimken li nekri shi tumubil
tqa da liya lisans?
فين يمكن لي نكري شي طمبيل؟
تقضي لي لصانص

How much is it daily/weekly?
shhal ktaddir f luym/ssimana?
شحل كتدير فاليوم/صيمنة؟

Where's the next petrol station?
fin kayna shi bumba dyal
lisans griba?
فين كاين شي بومبا ديال لصانص
قريب؟

I'd like ... litres please.
bghit ... itru 'afak
بغيت ... ايترو عفاك

Please check the ...	'afak shuf ...	... عفاك شوف
oil	zzit	زيت
water	lma	الماء

Can I park here?
wash nqder nwakef hna?
واش نقدر نوقف هنا؟

How long can I park here?
sh hal men waket neqder
nstatiun hna?
شحال من وقت نقدر نستشن
هناالطاكسيات قريبة من هنا؟

air	hawa	هواء
battery	lbatri	الباتري
boulevard	shariᶜ	شارع
brakes	lfranat	الفرنات
car	ṭōmubīl	طمبيل
clutch	vitas	فيتاس
dirt road	pīst	بيست
drivers licence	pirmi	برمي
engine	mutur	مطور
garage	lgarazh	الكراج
hire	kra	كرا
mechanic	mikanisyen	مكانيسيان
lights	dduw	ضو
oil	zzit	زيت
petrol	lişanş	ليسانص
puncture	pyasa	بيسة
radiator	rradyatur	رديانور
map	lkharita	خريطة
seatbelt	smta	سمتة
speed limit	Hed suur'a	حد السرعة
tyres	pnawat	بنوات
windscreen	barbriz	بربريز

Car Problems

We need a mechanic.
   khesna wahed lmikanisyan   خصنا واحد الميكانسيان

The car broke down at ...
   tumubil khasra f ...   طمبيل خسرة في ...

The battery is dead.
   lbatri khawi   الباتري خاوي

The radiator is leaking.
   kayqtter rradyatur   كيقطر رديانور

The car is overheating.
   tumubil skhnat bezaf   طمبيل صخنت بزاف

GETTING AROUND

I have a flat tyre.
  'ndi pyasa fruida
عندي بيسة فرويضة

It doesn't work.
  ma khddamash
ما خدماش

I lost my keys.
  ttudru liya swart
تضر لي سورت

BICYCLE

bicycle	beshklīṭ	بشكليت
motorcycle/moped	muṭur	مطور

Where can I hire a bicycle?
  fin yimken li nkri bshklit?
فين يمكن لي نقري بشكليت؟

How much is it for ...?	besh hal ghadi l ...?	بشحال غادي ل ...؟
an hour	sa'a	ساعة
the morning	lsabah	الصباح
the afternoon	lghita	الغيتة
the day	bel nhar	بالنهار

The tyre is flat.   ruida mghshuusha   رويضة مغشوشة

ACCOMMODATION

Hotels in Morocco are generally well furnished and reasonably priced. The majority are ranked using the European star system from one star (least expensive) to five star (most expensive). The prices of ranked hotels, except five star, are established by the government and are required by law to be posted. A list of all hotels and campsites is given out free of charge by the national tourist offices located in major cities.

When looking for accommodation you may be offered assistance by unofficial guides. Using a few Arabic phrases is a good way to let them know whether or not you need their services.

FINDING ACCOMMODATION

Where's a ...?	fīn kein ...?	فين كاين ... ؟
hotel	shī ūṭeil	شي اوطيل
Youth Hostel	'ūberzh, dār shshabab	اوبرج ، دارالشباب
campsite	shī mukheyyem	شي مخيم

I'm looking for	kanqelleb ʿala shī	قنقلب علي شي
a ... hotel.	ūṭeil ...	اوطيل ...
nice	mezyan	مزيان
clean	nqī	نقي
close	qrīb	قريب
cheap	rkheis	رخيص

What's the address?
ashnū hūwa lʿunwan? — اشنو هو العنوان؟

Please write down the address.
kteb lʿunwan ʿafek — اكتب لي العنوان عفاك

Please take me to a hotel.
weṣṣelnī l shī ūṭeil ʿafak — وصلني ل شي اوطيل عفاك

I've already found a hotel.
ana lgīt shī 'ūṭeil baʿda — انا لقيت شي اوطيل بعد

53

ACCOMMODATION

CHECKING IN

Is there a room available?
  wash kein shī bīt khawīya?

واش كاين شي بيت خاوي؟

I'd like to reserve a room.
  bghit uhzhez wahd lbit

بغيت احجز واحد البيت

What's the price of the room?
  shhal lttaman dyal lbīt?

شحل الّثمن ديال البيت؟

Is breakfast included?
  wash lfṭur mhsūb mʿa lbīt?

واش الفطور محسوب مع البيت؟

Which floor?
  ashmen ṭebqa?

اش من طبقة؟

I'd like a room …	bghit shī bīt …	بغيت شي بيت …
for one person	dyal wahed	ديال واحد
for two people	dyal zhūzh	ديال جوج
with a bathroom	belhammam	بالحمام
with a shower	beddūsh	بالدوج
with hot water	belma skhūn	بالماء سخن
that's clean	īkūn nqī	اكون نقي
that's peaceful	īkūn trunkīl	اكون مهدن

I'll be arriving at …
  ghādī nūwṣul fe …

غادي نوصل ف …

Can I see the room?
  wash yemkenli nshūf lbīt?

واش يمكن لي نشوف البيت؟

This room is good.
  had lbīt mezyana

هاد البيت مزيان

I don't like this room.
  maʿazhbnīsh had lbīt

ما عجبنيش هاد البيت

This room is dirty.
  had lbīt mwessekh

هاد البيت موسخ

DID YOU KNOW …   The word kif 'marijuana' is derived
from Arabic kayf, meaning 'pleasure'.

Is there a room available which is ... than this one?	wash kein shī bīt ... men hadī?	واش كاين شي بيت ... من هاد؟
bigger	kber	اكبر
smaller	ṣgher	اصغر
cheaper	rkheṣ	ارخص
better	hessen	حسن
cleaner	nqī	نقي

How much is a room for ...?	besh hal kein gbeit l ...?	بشحال كاين البيت ل...؟
one day	wahed nhar	واحد نهار
two days	yūmein	يومين
one week	wahed l'ūsbūʿ	واحد الاسبوع

I'm going to stay for ...
ghādī ngles ...

غادي نجلس ...

Is there hot water?
wash kein lma skhūn?

واش كاين الماء سخن؟

Is there a safe where I can leave my valuables?
wash ʾendkum shi kufrfur nhut
fih lhwayezh dyali lghalyeen?

واش عندكم شي كوفرفور نحط فيه الحوايج ديالي الغاليين؟

Should I pay now or later?
nkhelleṣ daba ʾuwla men bʿad?

نخلص دابا او لا من بعد؟

REQUESTS & QUERIES

Could we have an extra bed?
wash yemkenlek tzīdlīna
wahed nnamūsīya?

واش يمكنلك تزيدلينا واحد نموسية؟

Please bring me (a) ...	zhīblī ... ʿafak	جب لي ... عفاك
towel	wahed lfuta	واحد الفوطة
blanket	wahed lbṭānīya	واحد البطانية
breakfast	lfṭur	الفطور
bottled water	qerʿa dyal lma	القرعة ديال الماء

ACCOMMODATION

ACCOMMODATION

Which room is ours?
  ashmen bīt dyalna?
اش من بيت ديالنا؟

Please give me the room key.
  ʿaṭienī ṣṣārūt dyal bīt ʿafak
عطيني ساروت ديال البيت عفاك

I've lost my room key.
  tudder liya ssarut dyal lbit dyali
توضر لي ساروت ديال البيت ديالي

Where can I wash my clothes?
  fīn yemkenlī nṣebben hwayezhī?
فين يمكن لي نصبن حوايجي؟

Please clean the room now.
  neḍḍeflī lbīt daba ʿafak
نضف لي البيت داب عفاك

Can I make a telephone call?
  wash yemkenlī nʿmel telefun?
واش امكن لي نعمل تليفون؟

Do you change money here?
  wash katserrfū lflus?
واش كتصرفو الفلوس؟

Can I leave a message?
  wash nqder nkhlli shi wasaya?
واش نقدر نخلي شي وصاية؟

Is there a message for me?
  wash kain shi wasaya dyali?
واش كاين شي وصاية ديالي؟

Please wake me at 7:00.
  fiyaqni ʾafak f sab'a
فيقني عفاك ف سبعة

Can I change to another room?
  wash yemken li nthuwwel l
  bit akhar?
واش يمكن لي نتحول لبيت اخر؟

Please ... this for me.	ʿafak ... līya hada	عفاك ... لي هادا
wash	ṣebben	صبن
iron	sleh	صلح
sew	kheyyeṭ	خيط

When will it be ready?
  ʾemta ghādī tkūn mūzhūda?
امتي غادي تكون موجودة؟

I need it today/tomorrow.
  ana mehtazh bīha lyūm/ghedda
انا محتاج بها اليوم / غدا

I need it quickly.
    ana zerban bīha
انا زربان بها

This isn't mine.
    hadī mashī dyalī
هادي ماشي ديالي

Is the laundry ready?
    wash lhwayezh wazhdīn?
واش الحوايج واجدين؟

COMPLAINTS

The ... doesn't work.	l ... khasser/ma khedemsh	ال...خاسر / ماخدامش
air-conditioning	lklimasyiun	لكليمايزيون
heating	shehd	شهد
electricity/lights	trisinti/duw	تريسيتي / الضو
key	ssarut	الساروت
shower	ddush	الحمام / الدوش
toilet	bit lma	بيت الماء
plumbing	taplumbit	تبلمبيت

Please fix it.
    ʾafak suwebu/suwebha
عفاك صوبو / صوبها

Someone came into my room.
    dkhel shīwahed felbīt dyalī
دخل شي واحد فالبيت ديالي

Something was stolen from my room.
    tserreq shīhazha men bīt dyalī
تسرق شي حاجة من البيت ديالي

I'm locked out of my room.
    tshed ʾliya lbab dyal
    lbit dyali men berra
تشد علي الباب ديال البيت
ديالي من علي برا

ACCOMMODATION

This room is too ...	had lbīt ... bezzaf	هاد البيت ... بزاف
hot	skhūn	سخون
cold	berḍ	بارد
loud	feha ṣdaʿ	فيها الصداع
expensive	ghalī	غالي

This ... is dirty	had ... mwessekh	هاد ... موسخ
blanket	kashsha/bttaniya	البطانية / الكاشة
sheet	lizar	لزار
pillow case	lghassa dyal lmkhda	الغسة ديال المخدة
pillow	mkhdda/khddiya	المخدة / خدية

Please change it.
   beḍḍelha ʿafak   بدلها عفاك

The window won't open.
   lsherzhem makeihelsh   الشرجم ما كيهلش

CHECKING OUT

We'd like to check out ...	bghīna nemshī ...	بغينا نمشي ...
now	daba	داب
at noon	feṭṭnash	ف الطناش
tomorrow	ghedda	غدا
tomorrow morning	ghedda feṣṣbah	غدا ف الصباح

Please prepare the bill.
   wezhedlīna lhsab ʿafak   وجد لنا الحساب عفاك

Can I pay by ...?	wash yemkenlī nkhelleṣ b ...?	واش يمكن لي نخلص ب ...؟
travellers cheque	shek sīyahī	الشيك السياحي
credit card	kārt krīdī	كارت كريدي

You made a mistake in the bill.
   ghulṭō fel hsab   غلطو ف الحساب

I've already paid.
   khulluṣt men qbel   خلصت من قبل

Can I leave my things here until this afternoon/evening?
wash yemkenlī nkhellī lhaweyzh dyalī henna hetta had
lᶜshīya/illīl?

واش يمكن لي نخلي الحوايج ديالي هنا حتى هاد العشية / الليل؟

Call me a taxi please.
ᶜyyetlī ᶜla ṭṭāksī ᶜafak

عيطلي علي طاكسي عفاك

Where's the laundry?
fin keina shī meṣbana?

فين كاينة شي مصبانة؟

ACCOMMODATION

Useful Words

address	ᶜunwan	عنوان
air-conditioning	klematīzasīyun	كليماتيزاسيون
arrival	wṣul	وصول
ashtray	tfeia	طفاية
balcony	balkun	البلكون
bathtub	hammam	حمام
bed	namūsīya	الناموسية
bedroom	bīt nnᶜas	بيت نعاس
blanket	bṭṭānīya	البطانية / الكاشة
chair	kūrsī	الكرسي
clean	nqī	نقي
cold	berd	برد
cost	taman	الثمن
crowded	zham	زحام
curtain	khamīya	الخامية
dinner	ᶜsha	العشاء
dirty	mwessekh	موسخ
door	bab	الباب
electricity	ḍō	الضو
empty	khawī	خاوي
food	makla	المكلة
full	ᶜamer	عامر

ACCOMMODATION

Useful Words

lift (n)	sensūr	سانسور
light bulb	būla	البولة
lock	qfel	القفل
mattress	mddreba	المضربة
mirror	mreiya	المراية
noise	ṣḍaʿ	صداع
pillow	mkhedda	مخدة
quiet	mhedden	مهدن
room	bīt	البيت
sheet	īzar	يزار
shower	dúzh	الدوش
sleep	naʿsa	نعاس
soap	ṣābūn	صابون
spend the night	bat	بات
stairs	drūzh	دروج
suitcase	balīza	باليزة
table	tâbla	طابلة
toilet	bīt lma	بيت الماء
toilet paper	kaghit dyal bit lma	كاغيط ديال بيت الماء
towel	futa	فوطة
water	lma	الماء
window	sherzhem	السرجم

AROUND TOWN

LOOKING FOR ...

The quickest way to get oriented in a Moroccan city is to head directly for the local tourist office. They are normally located in the centre of town and offer free city maps which include the main municipal buildings and tourist sites.

When looking for a particular address you could run into trouble. Often streets and numbers are unmarked and many street names, especially in Casablanca and Rabat, have recently been changed from French to Arabic. The best bet is to ask a local shop owner if you suspect the address is nearby. If all else fails, the unofficial experts in giving directions are the small (petit) taxi drivers.

Where is a/the ...?	fīn kein ...?	فين كان ... ؟
bank	shī bānka	شي بنكة
barber	shī hellaq	شي حلاق
bathroom	lbīt lma	البيت الماء
laundry	shī mṣebbana	شي مصبنة
market	lmarshei	المارشي
open air market	ssūq	السوق
old city	lmdīna lqdīma	المدينة القديمة
police station	lkūmīsarīya	الكوميسارية
post office	lbūstā	البوسطة
town hall	lbaladīya	البلدية
... embassy	ssifara dyal ...	السفارة ديال ...
... consulate	lqunṣūlīya dyal ...	القنصلية ديال ...

How far is ...?
  shhal b°eid ...?

شحال بعيد؟

What time do they open?
  weqtash keihellū?

وقتاش كيحلو؟

What time do they close?
  weqtash keiseddū?

وقتاش كيسدو؟

Are they still open?
  wash mazel halīn?

واش مازال حالين؟

AT THE BANK

After bargaining for almost every purchase, you'll be pleased to find that currency exchange rates are fixed by the government and will be the same wherever you change money. Rates are posted, although a few banks have started charging a fee for changing travellers cheques.

Banking hours for most of the year are 8.30 to 11.30 am and 2.15 to 4.15 pm. During Ramadan (the Muslim month of fasting) and summer months, the hours change to 8.15 am to 1.45 pm. At other times, money can be changed at the international airports and most major hotels.

The dirham, Morocco's currency, cannot be exchanged once you're out of the country. Save your exchange receipts because you can change a percentage back into foreign currency at the airport when you leave.

I'd like to exchange some money.
  bghīt nṣerref shī flūs

بغيت نصرف شي فلوس

Has my money arrived yet?
  wash weslu lflūs dyalī awla mazel?

واش وصلو الفلوس اولا مزال؟

When will my money arrive?

'emta ghādī īwṣul lflūs dyalī?   امتى غادي يوصلو الفلوس ديالي؟

Where should I sign?

fin kheṣṣnī nweqqī'?   فين خصني نوقع؟

Can I have money transferred here from my bank?

wash yemken llbanka dyalī   واش يمكن للبنك ديالي
thawel shī flūs lhenna?   تحول شي فلوس لهنا؟

How long will it take for the money to arrive?

shhal keikheṣṣ dyal   شحال كيخص ديال الوقت
wekt lhqu lflus?   الحكو الفلوس؟

I'd like to get some money with my credit card.

bhīt nakhūd shī flūs   بغيت نخرج شي فلوس
belkart krīdī   بالكارت كريدي

Useful Words

banknotes	wraq	وراق
cash window	ṣenduq	صندوق
change	ṣerf	صرف
money	flūs	فلوس
travellers cheque	shek sīyahī	الشيك السياحي

AROUND TOWN

AT THE POST OFFICE

Stamps are available at tobacco stands as well as at the post office. It's best to mail your letters at the mail slots outside post offices, as pick-ups can be infrequent at other mail boxes. Sending packages out of the country is fairly straightforward, although you'll be asked to fill out a customs declaration form. Be sure to leave the package open because an official has to see the contents before it's sealed.

I'd like to ...   bghīt ...   ... بغيت
   buy some stamps   nshrī shī tnaber   نشري شي تنابر
   send a telegram   nṣeifeṭ waḥed ttīlīgram   نصيفط واحد التليجرام
   send a package   nṣeifeṭ waḥed lkūlīya   نصيفط واحد الكولية
   send this   nṣeifeṭ hadī recūmāndei   نصيفط هد ركومندي
    registered mail

How much is it to send this to ...?
   bshḥal ghādī ... nṣeifeṭhadī l?   بشحال غادي... نصيفط هد ل؟

How much is it to send a postcard to (the USA)?
   bshḥal ghādī nṣeifeṭ waḥed lkart pustāl l(amrīka)?

بشحال غادي نصيفط واحد الكارت بوسطال ل (المريك)؟

I want to send   bghīt nṣeifeṭ   بغيت نصيفط
this by ...   hadī ...   ... هد
   air mail   betteiyyāra   بالطيارة
   surface post   ʿadīya   عادية
   express mail   bekspres   باكسبرس

Please give me a receipt.
   ʿṭeinī fakṭura ʿafak   عطيني الفاكتورة عفاك
Has any mail come for me?
   wash zhawlīya shī brāwat?   واش جاولي شي براوات؟

Useful Words

box	şenduq	الصندوق
breakable	ítherres	اتهرس
cardboard box	kartūna	الكارتونة
customs official	dīwānī	الديواني
envelope	zhwa	جوي
glue	lşāq	لصاق
inspector	mūfettīsh	المفتش
insurance	lāşurānş	لصورانص
mailman	faktur	فاكتور
number	raqem	رقم
pen	stīlū	الستيلو
phone stall in post office	bīt	بيت
stamp	tanber	التامبر
string	qennba	القنبة
tape	skātsh	السكتش
wrapping paper	kaghīt	كاغيط

TELECOMMUNICATIONS

For telephone calls, phone booths located throughout major cities are far and away the best choice. For anything other than local calls, they are much cheaper than hotels and always quicker than the post office. Reverse charge calls can be made either from a hotel or the phone section of the post office. State that you wish to call 'PCV' and provide your name as well as the name, city, country and number of the person you're calling.

I'd like to use the telephone please.
    bghī nduwer ttelefūn'afak   بغيت نضور التلفون عفاك
I want to call ...
    bghit n'eyyett ...   بغيت نعيط . . .

Here's the number.
ha raqem

هاالرقم

How much per minute?
shhal ldqiqa?

شحال ل دقيقة؟

I want to make a reverse charge phone call.
bghīt n'mel ttelefūn PCV

بغيت نضور التلفون ب س ف

It's busy.
mshghul

مشغول

I've been cut off.
ttqtte' lkhett 'liyya

تقطع لخط علي

It's ringing.
tayserser

تيسرسر

What's the area code for ...?
ashu huw landikatif dyal ...?

اشو هو لندكتيف ديال ...؟

AROUND TOWN

Making a call

Hello. (answering a call)
allu

الو

Who's calling?
shkūn?

شكون؟

It's ...
hadā/hadī ...

هدا / هدي ...

Is ... there?
wash kain ...?

واش كاين ...؟

Yes, he's/she's here.
iyyeh, kain/kaina hna

اية ، كاين / كاينة هنا

One moment.
  wahed shwiyya
  واحد شوي

He/she isn't here.
  makain/makainash hna
  ماكاين/ماكايناش هنا

What time will he/she return?
  imta gha yerzhe'/gha terzha'?
  امتي غادي ارجع / ترجع؟

I want to leave a message.
  bghit nkhlli wahd lmessazh
  بغيت نخلي واحد المساج

Please tell her I called.
  'afak gulleha rani hddert
  عفاك كولها رني هضرت

I'll call back later.
  ghadi b'ayet men ba'd
  غادي بعيط من بعد

SIGHTSEEING

Where's the tourist office?
  fin kain mktab dyal ssiyaha?
  فين مكتب ديال السياحة؟

Do you have a local map?
  wash kain 'andek lkharitta
  dyal mdina?
  واش كاين عندك الخاريطة ديال المدينة؟

I'd like to see ...
  bghit nshuf ...
  بغيت نشوف ...

cinema	lssinima	السينما
beach	bher	بحر
crowded	zham	زحام
market	l marshi	المارشي
mosque	zhzhame'	الجامع
parade	isti'rad	استعراض
park	'arsa	عرصة
university	lzhami'a	الجامعة

AROUND TOWN

What's this building?
  ash katkun had lbinaya?

اش كتكون هد البناية؟

How much does it cost to get in?
  shhal ttaman dyal ddekhla?

شحال الثمن ديال الدخلة؟

May I take a photograph?
  wash yimken lli nākhud
  shi tssewwera?

واش يمكن لي نخذ شي تصورة؟

I'll send you a photograph.
  ghadi s°feit wahed tssewwera

غادي صفت واحد تصورة

Please take a photograph of me.
  swarni ʾafak

صورني عفاك

AROUND TOWN

COMMON INTERESTS

What do you do in your spare time?

'ash katdīr felweqt lfaragh dyalek? | اش كتدير فالوقت الفراغ ديالك؟

| I like ... | kei'zhebnī ... | ... كيعجبني |
| I don't like ... | makei'zhebnīsh ... | ... ماكيعجبنيش |

Do you like ...?	wash kat'zhebek ...?	... واش كيعجبك
art	lfin	الفن
cooking	tteyyeb	التطيب
dancing	shshtīh	الشطيح
films	l'aflam	الافلام
music	lmūsīqa	الموسيقى
playing soccer	tl'ab kōra	تلعب الكرة
playing sports	tdīr rrīyada	دير الرياضة
reading books	tqra' lkūb	تقراء الكتب
shopping	ttessewuq	التسوق
travelling	tesafer	التسافر
watching TV	tferrezh fettelfaza	تفرج في تلفزة
writing	tekteb	تكتب

SPORT

Do you like to play sport?

wash kei'zebek tdīr rrīyada? | واش كيعجبك تدير الرياضة؟

I like playing sport.

'zīz 'līya ndīr rrīyada | عزيز علي ندير الرياضة

I prefer to watch, not play.

kanfeḍḍel ntferrezh ū manl'absh | كنفضل نتفرج و ما نلعبش

Do you play ...?

wash kat l'ab ...? | واش كتلعب ...؟

Would you like to (play) ...?	wash bghīti tlʿab ...?	واش بغيت تلعب ... ؟
basketball	lbasket	الباسكيط
box	lbōks	البوكس
exercise	rrīyyaḍa	الرياضة
football	lkura	الكرة
hockey	lhōkī	الهوكي
rugby	rrōgbī	الركبي
ski	tzhlīq	تزحليق
surf	sserf	السورف
swim	ʿōman	العومان
tennis	tīnnīs	التنيس

FAMILY

This is my ...	hada ... (m)	هدا ...
	hadī ... (f)	هدي ...
wife	mrātī	مراتي
husband	razhlī	راجلي
brother	khuya	خوي
sister	khutī	خوتي
mother	mmwī/lwalīda dyalī	امي / الوالدة ديالي
father	bba/lwalīd dyalī	با / الوالد ديالي
parents	waldīya	والدي
son	weldī	ولدي
daughter	bentī	بنتي
friend	ṣāhbī (m)	صاحبي
	ṣāhbtī (f)	صاحبتي

INTERESTS

Are you married?
   wash nta mzhūwzh? (m)   واش انت مزوج؟
   was nti mzhūwzha? (f)   واش انت مزوجة؟

I'm married.
   ana mzhūwzh (m)   انا مزوج
   ana mzhūwzha (f)   انا مزوجة

I'm not married.
   ana mamzhūwzhsh (m)   انا ما مزوج
   ana mamzhūwzhash (f)   انا ما مزوجة

Do you have any children?
   wash ʿandek lūwlad?   واش عندك الولاد؟

I don't have any children.
   mʿandīsh lūwlad   ماعنديش الولاد

How many children do you have?
   shhal men weld ʿandek?   شحال من ولد عندك؟

I have ...	ʿandī ...	... عندي
one daughter	wahed lbent	واحد البنت
two daughters	zhūzh dyal lbnat	جوج بنات
one son	wahed lweld	واحد الولد
two sons	zhūzh dyal lūwlad	جوج ولاد

HOBBIES

Do you have any hobbies?
   wash ʿandek shī hiwya?   واش عندك شي هواية؟

I like to ...	ʿazīz ʿalīya ...	... عزيز علي
cook	nṭeyyeb	نطيب
draw	nṣewwer	نصور
garden	lbastana	البستنة
sew	nkhīyyeṭ	نخيط
travel	nsafer	نسافر

I collect ...	kanzhmaʿ ...	... كنجمع
books	lktūb	الكتب
coins	ṣṣerf	صرف
stamps	ttnaber	تنابر

INTERESTS

STAYING IN TOUCH

I'm leaving tomorrow.
ghadī nemshī ghedda

غادي نمشي غدا

Let's stay in touch.
khellīna ntshawfū

خلينا نتشاوفو

Let's swap addresses.
yallah ntbadlū lʿanawīn

يالاه نتبادلو العناوين

Do you have a pen and paper?
wash ʿandek stīlū ū werqa?

واش عندك ستيلو و ورقة؟

Here's my address.
ha lʿunwan dyalī

ها العنوان ديالي

What's your address?
ashnū lʿunwan dyalek?

اشنو العنوان ديالك؟

If you ever come to ... you're welcome at my house.
īla zhītī ... marhaba bīk f dārī

الي جيتي ... مرحب بك ف داري

Don't forget to write.
matnsash tkteb

ما تنساش تكتب

I'll send you copies of the pictures.
ghadī nṣeftlek teṣṣawer

غادي نصيفت لك تصاور

It was great meeting you.
ana ferhan bash nʿarfek

انا فرحان باش نعارفك

Morocco is a shopper's paradise. From exotic tribal jewellery to herbal cures, almost anything imaginable can be found in Morocco's markets (souqs). Every price is open for negotiation and bargaining is expected. Moroccan shop owners are known for their shrewdness so when haggling be prepared to match wits with some of the best. Using Arabic should allow you to not only have some fun but also get a better price.

LOOKING FOR

Where is a/an ...?	fīn kein ...?	فين كاين . . . ؟
bakery	fārrān	فران
barber	Hāllāk	حلاق
bookshop	shī mektaba	شي مكتبة
butcher	zhezzār	جزار
chemist/pharmacy	lfarmāsiyān	الفارماسيان
grocery shop	shī hanūt	شي حانوت
hardware shop	shī drūgrī	شي دروكري
laundry	māsbānā	مصبنة
open air market	ssūq	السوق
souvenir shop	bāzaar	بزار
tobacco shop	shī ṣṣakka	شي صاكة
travel agency	wekālet el āsfār	وكالة الاسفار
vegetable market	lmarshei	المارشي

SHOPPING

Do you have ...?	wash ʿandkom ...?	واش عندكم ...؟
English newspapers	zhzharaʾīd bneglīzīya	جرايد بنكليزية
film	lfīlm	الفيلم
a sheet of paper	wahed lwerqa	واحد الورقة
stamps	ttnaber	تنابر

Where can I buy ...?	fin ghādī neshrī ...?	فين يمكن لي نشتري ...؟
soap	ṣṣābon	الصابون
maps	lkhārāʾīt	الخرايط
pens	sstīlūwat	الستيلوات
pencils	lqlūma	القلوم

MAKING A PURCHASE

I'd like to buy ...
　bghīt nshrī ...　　　　　　　　　　بغيت نشري ...
Do you have anything else?
　wash ʿandkom shī hazha akhora?　واش عندكم شي حاجة اخري؟
I don't like it.
　maʿzhebatnīsh　　　　　　　　　ما عجبتنيش
Can I look at it?
　wakhkha nshūfha?　　　　　　　واش نقدر نشوفها؟
I'm only looking.
　ghīr kanshūf　　　　　　　　　غير كنشوف
How much is it?
　bshhal?　　　　　　　　　　　بشحال؟

SHOPPING

Please write down the price.

ktеb ttaman ʿafak

كتب التمن عفاك

Can I pay by credit card?

wash nkder nkhelleṣ bel
kart kredī?

واش نقدر نخلص باكرت كريدي؟

Please wrap it.

zhmaʿha li ʿafak

جمعها لي عفاك

BARGAINING

Bargaining is an art in Morocco and is practised for almost every purchase. In fact, sellers will sometimes seem disappointed if you pay without an argument. To determine a fair starting price for an item in the souqs, you might try checking the same item at several different shops before zeroing in on the one you want. Depending on the item, offer an amount significantly below the price and see how quickly it drops.

The phrases below are most effective when said as if you're insulted the price is so high. Sometimes stomping away from the seller until he asks you to return also works. If you wish to maximise your bargaining position, avoid buying anything while you are with a 'guide'. They often receive a large percentage and thus inflate the prices.

How much?

bshhal?

بشحال؟

It's too much for me.

bezzaf ʿliya

بزاف علي

That's very expensive.

ghalī bezzaf

غالي بزاف

Give me a reasonable price please.

dīr mʿaya wahed ttaman
meʿqol ʿafak

دير معاي واحد التمن معقول عفاك

What's the last price?

akhīr taman shhal?

اخر تمن اشحال؟

That's my last price.

akhīr ttaman dyalī hūwa hada

اخر التمن ديالي هو هد

SHOPPING

Is there one cheaper than this?

wash kein wahed rkheiṣ ‘la hada?   واش كاين شي واحد رخيص علي هد؟

ESSENTIAL GROCERIES

Where can I find ...?	fīn ghādī nelqa ...?	فين نقدر نلق ...؟
I'd like to buy (a) ...	bghīt neshrī ...	بغيت نشري ...
batteries	lнāzhārāt	الحجرات
bread	lkhōbz	الخبز
butter	lzebdā	الزبدة
cheese	lfromāzh	الفرماج
chocolate	lchoklāt	الشكلاط
eggs	lbeyd	البيض
flour	dakīk	دكيك
gas cylinder	lbootā dyāl lghaz	البوطة ديال الغاز
honey	l‘āsāl	العسل
jam	kōfitir	كوفيتير
laundry soap	lsāboon dyal tzbīn	الصابون ديال تصبين
margarine	marzharīn	مرجارين
matches	lwākd	لوقد
milk	lнālīb	الحليب
olives	lzeitoon	الزيتون
pepper	lfleflā	الفلفلة
salt	lmelhā	الملحة
shampoo	shampwān	شمبوان
soap	lsāboon	الصابون
sugar	lsūkār	السكر

toilet paper	kāghīt	كاغيط
toothpaste	ldantifrīs	الدنتفريس
yoghurt	yōkort	يوكرت

SHOPPING

SOUVENIRS & HANDICRAFTS

bag/purse	sak	صاك
basket	sella	سلة
blanket	bṭṭāniya	بطانية
brass	nhas ṣfer	النحاس الاصفر
carpet	zerbīya	الزربية
copper	lnhas lhmer	النحاس الحمر
cup/glass	lkas	الكاس
embroidery	ṭerz	طرز
leather	zheld	جلد
mirror	mraya	المراية
pitcher	ghorraf	غراف
plate	ṭebṣel	الطبسل
pottery	fekhkhar	الفخار
tray	ṣeinīya	الصينية
vase/pot	mhebbeq	المحبق

CLOTHING

Do you have one in my size?

wash ʿendeq shi wahed
fltaqadda dyali?

واش عندك شي واحد ف التقد ديالي؟

Five in Your Eye

Depictions of the hand of Fatima (daughter of Mohammed) or
the number 5, often found on jewellery, are believed to have
the same effect as poking the fingers in the evil eye when used
with the words khamsa fi ainek, 'five in your eye'.

SHOPPING

Can I try it on?
    wash neqder neshrbo?   واش نقدر نجربو؟
It fits well.
    zha m'aya huwa hadak   جا معاي هو هداك
It doesn't fit.
    mashash m'aya   ما جاش معاي

It's too ...	hada ... bezzaf	هدا ... بزاف
big	kbīr	كبير
small	ṣgheir	صغير
long	ṭwīl	طويل
short	qṣīr	قصير
tight	mzīr	مزير
loose	translit	عريض

Do you have this in any other colours?
    wash kein hada b shī lūn akhōr?   واش كاين هد ب شي لون اخر؟
Can you alter this?
    wash tqder thiyyid hāda?   واش تقدر تحيد هد؟
When will it be ready?
    'emta ghādī īkūn mūzhūd?   امتي غادي اكون موجود؟

boots	botīyon	بوطيون
bra	ssūtyīm	سوتيام
coat	lkbōt	الكبوط
dress	kswā	كسوة
hat	ṭerbūsh	الطربوش
jacket	kebboṭ	كبوط
pants	serwal	السروال
shirt	lqamīzha	القميجة
shoes	lṣebbaṭ	الصباط
socks	tqasher	تقاشر
sports shoes	ṣberdīla	سبرديلا
sweater	trīkū	تريكو
swimsuit	hwayezh d l'umān	حوايج دالعومان
T-shirt	tīshūrt	تي شورت
umbrella	lmddel	المضل
underwear	slīp	السليب

COLOURS

dark	meghlūq	مغلوق
light	meftūh	مفتوح
white	byeḍ	بيض
black	khel	كحل
blue	zreq	زرق
brown	qehwi	قهوي
green	khder	خضر
grey	rmadī	رمادي
red	hmer	حمر
yellow	ṣfer	صفر

SHOPPING

TOILETRIES

after-shave/perfume	rīha	الريحة
deodorant	dyodoron	ديودرون
razor	zezwar	الزيزوار
shampoo	shampwan	شمبوان
soap	ṣābōn	الصابون
sun block	lomber	لمبر
tampons	fota dyal dem lhīd	فوطة ديال دم الحيض
toothbrush	shīṭa dyal ssnan	الشيتة ديال السنان
toothpaste	mᶜzhūn dyal ssnan	معجون ديال سنان
toilet paper	kaghīt dyal bīt lma	كغيط ديال بيت الماء

SHOPPING

FOR THE BABY

baby food	makla dyal drrī sghīr	مكلة ديال دري صغير
baby powder	ttalk	الطالك
bib	ryaka	الرياكة
disposable nappies	lkhrūk	الخروق
dummy/pacifier	lskāta	السكاتة
feeding bottle	lrddaᶜā	الرضاعة
nappy/diaper	lkhrūq	الخروق
nappy rash cream	lpomād	البوماد
powdered milk	Hlīb dyal lghbrā	الحليب ديال الغبرة
formula	farina dyal drari sghār	فرينة ديال دراري صغار

STATIONERY & PUBLICATIONS

Is there an English language bookshop here?
    wash kayna shī mktaba dyal nglīziya hna?

واش كاين شي مكتبة ديال نكليزية هنا؟

Do you have an English language section?
    wash ᶜendkom lktūb dyal lngliziya?

واش عنكم الكتوب ديال النكليزية؟

Do you sell ...?	wash katbīᶜū ...?	واش كنبيعو . . . ؟
books	lektub	الكتب
magazines	lmazhellat	المجلات
newspapers	zhzhara'id	الجرايد
paper	lwurak	الوراق

postcards	lekart postal	لكارت بوسطال
envelopes	zhzhwa	جوي
stamps	ttnaber	التنابر
pens	sstīlowat	ستيلوات
pencils	leqlam	القلام
city maps	lkhrayet dyal lmdina	خرايط ديال المدينة
road maps	lkhrayet dyal trqan	خرايط ديال طرقان

MUSIC

I'm looking for a ...	kanqelleb ʿla ...	كنقلب علي ...
CD	dīsk llazer	ديسك لايزر
cassette tape	kasīt dyal lmūsazhela	كسط ديال المسجلة

| traditional | teqlīdī | تقليدي |
| modern | ʿessrī | عصري |

Please recommend some Moroccan music.

ʿafak khtar li shi mūsika maghrebīya

عفاك ختارلي شي موسيقي مغربية

Do you have any ...?   wash ʿendek shi ...?   واش عندك شي ... ؟

Can I listen to this here?

wash yimken lī nsmeʿ lhadī hna?

واش يمكن لي نسمع ل هد هنا؟

I need a blank tape.

khsnī kassīt khawiya

خصني كسيط خاوية

PHOTOGRAPHY

How much is it to process this film?

bshhāl tнmīd dyal hada lfilm?

بشحال تحميض ديال هد الفيلم؟

SHOPPING

When will it be ready?

imta ghadī ykūn mwezhūd?   امتي غادي يكون موجود؟

I'd like a film for this camera please.

bghīt wahed lfilm lhad
sssawara ʿafak   بغيت واحد الفيلم لهد صورة عفاك

Can you install this film please?

wash tqder tweshshed liya had   واش تقدر توجد لي هد الفيلم عفاك؟
lfilm ʿafak?

I'd like some passport photos please.

bghīt shī tsawer dyāl
lpaspor ʿafak   بغيت شي تصاور ديال البسبورت عفاك

My camera doesn't work.

sūra dyali khāsrā   صورة ديالي خاسرة

The film is jammed.

lfilm khser   الفيلم خسر

The battery is dead.

lнzhrā mmiyta   الحجرة ميتة

Do you have a battery for this camera?

wash ʿendek shī hzhra dyal   واش عندك شي حجرة ديال هد صورة؟
had ssowara?

battery	нzhrā	حجرة
black & white	lbyḍ ū lkhel	البيض و الكحل
colour	llūn	اللون
film	film	فيلم
film speed	surʿet lfilm	سرعة الفيلم
flash	flāsh	فلاش
lens	zhzhazhat	ججات
video tape	kassīt vī dyo	كاصيط فيديو

WEIGHTS & MEASURES

gram	gram	كرام
kilogram	kīlū	كيلو
metre	mītrū	ميترو
centimetre	şāntīm	سنتيم
litre	lītro	ليترو
half a litre	ness leetro	نص ليترو
a little bit	shī shwīya	شي شوية

SIZES & COMPARISONS

big	kbīr	كبير
bigger than this	kber men hada	كبر من هدا
too big for me	kbīr 'līya	كبير علي
small	şghīr	صغير
smaller than this	şgher men hada	صغير من هد
too small for me	şghīr 'līya	صغير علي
tight	mzeyyer	مزير
long	twīl	طويل
many/a lot/too much	bezzaf	بزاف

Polite Forms of Address

Polite forms of address, roughly equivalent to Mr, Mrs and Ms are sī, asīdī and alalla, followed by a first name. In return you may be addressed as 'Mr Max' or 'Mrs Sandra'.

SHOPPING

SHOPPING

a little bit	shwīya	شوي
enough	baraka	بارك
like/the same	bhal bhal	بحال بحال
heavy	tqīl	تقيل
light	khfif	خفيف

MOROCCAN HOSPITALITY

One of the most important ingredients of the national cuisine is the gracious and hospitable atmosphere of the Moroccan home. If you're invited for a meal, here are some things to keep in mind. First, shoes are not normally worn inside so you'll be expected to remove yours before stepping on any carpets. Don't worry about washing your hands, your host will bring a basin with water to you while you're seated.

Once the host pronounces besmīllah, 'in the name of God', the meal will begin with everyone eating out of a common dish with their hands or, if kūskūs is served, possibly with spoons. The meat will be in the centre of the dish under vegetables and is eaten last, often being divided and distributed by the host. Don't eat too much because what often appears to be the main course will actually be the first of two or three! Be ready for some strong encouragement to continue eating even after you're full – your host wants to make sure you feel welcome. The phrase llah yzh^ca lbaraka, 'may God bring (you) a blessing', is a polite way of saying you've had enough.

MEALS

We would like to have ...	bghīna ...	... بغينا
breakfast	nfeṭru	نفطرو
lunch	nteghddaw	نتغداو
dinner	nt^cshaw	نتعشو

VEGETARIAN & SPECIAL MEALS

I don't eat meat.
makanakūlsh lhem أنا ماكنكولش اللحم

I don't eat chicken, fish or pork.
makanakūlsh dzhazh, lhōt ماكنكولش ادجاج لا الحوت ولا الحلوف
awla hlūf

I don't eat dairy products.
　　makanakūlsh makla lī fīhā halīb　　　　ماكنكولش مكلة لي فيها الحليب

Do you have anything without meat?
　　wash kein shī hazha bla lham?　　　　واش كاين شي حاجة بلا اللحم؟

Bring me this without meat please.
　　zhīblī hadī bla lham 'afak　　　　جيب لي هد بلا اللحم عفاك

Does this contain egg?
　　wash fīha lbeiḍ?　　　　واش فيها البيض؟

I'm allergic to ...
　　fīya wed hasasīya dyal ...　　　　عندي الحساسية ديال ...

I can't eat ...　　manqdersh nakūl ...　　　　ما نقدرش نكول ...
　　meat　　　　lhem　　　　اللحم
　　eggs　　　　lbeiḍ　　　　البيض
　　sugar　　　　ssūkkar　　　　سكر
　　chickpeas　　Hums　　　　حمص

EATING OUT

We would like a table for four please.
　　bghīna wahed ṭṭābla dyal
　　rbeᶜa 'afak　　　　بغينا واحد الطبلة ديال الربع عفاك

Please bring me　　'afak zhiblī ...　　　　عفاك جبلي ...
the/a(n) ...
　　menu　　　　lmīnū　　　　المينو
　　glass of water　　wahed lkas dyal lma　　واحد الكاس ديال الماء
　　ash tray　　teffaya　　　　طفاية
　　bill　　　　lhsab　　　　الحساب

FOOD

bread	khebz	خبز
fork	lfershetta	لفيرشطة
knife	lmūs	لموس
spoon	lᶜashek	لعاشق
napkin	lkālᶜ	القلع
plate	tabstel	طبستل
pepper	lebrwa	لبراو
salt	melнa	ملحة

Do you have ...?
    wash ᶜendkem ...? واش عندكم ...؟

Is service included in the bill?
    wash sserbīs dakhel felhsab? واش سربيس داخل ف الحساب؟

What do you recommend?
    Ash ghā tekhtār lī? اش غا تخطار لي؟

What are they eating?
    Ash kayaklū? اش كيكلو؟

I would like what those people are eating.
    bghīt hadakeshi lkyaklū بغيت هدكشي لكيكلو هدوك الناس
    hadūk lnās

What's in this?
    Ash kein f hada? اش كاين ف هد؟

This is delicious.
    hada bnīn هدا بنين

This isn't cooked well enough.
    hadī maṭeibash mezyan هد ما طيباش مزيان

Utensils

cup/glass	kas	كاس
fork	fershetta	فرشيطة
knife	mūs	موس
plate	ṭebṣeil	طبيسل
spoon	mᶜelqa	معلقة

FOOD

FOOD

Useful Words

boiled	mslūq	مسلوق
bottle	qerʿa	قرعة
clean	nqī	نقي
cold	bared	بارد
delicious	bnīn	بنين
dirty	mwessekh	موسخ
empty	khawī	خاوي
fresh	trei	طري
fried	meqlī	مقلي
full	ʿamer	عامر
hot	skhūn	سخون
hot (spicy)	harr	حار
rare	maṭeiybsh bezzef	خضر
raw	ghḍer	غدر
ripe	tayeb	طايب
roasted	meshwī	مشوي
rotten	ghamezh	خامج
sour/unseasoned	mssūs	مسوس
stale	qdīm	قديم
sweet	hlew	حلو
warm	dafī	دافي
well done	teiyeb mezyan	طايب مزيان

STREET FOOD

An amazing variety of prepared food is offered by street vendors and in small stalls and shops throughout Morocco. Typically you'll find them wherever crowds gather, for example, Djemaa-el-Fna in Marrakesh, or near train and bus stops.

What's that?		
	shnū hadak?	شنو هدك؟
What's in it?		
	ash kein fīha f ldakhel?	اش كاين فيها ف الداخل؟
What's he eating?		
	ash keiyakūl?	اش كياكل؟
Please give me what he's eating.		
	ʿaṭeinī dakshī lī kayakūl hadak	عطيني هد كشي لي كياكول هدك
Please give me a taste.		
	ʿaṭeinī wahed ḍūka 'afak	عطيني ندوق عفاك
Please give me a little bit.		
	ʿaṭeinī wahed shwīya 'afak	عطيني واحد شوي عفاك
We'd like to try that.		
	bghīna nzherrebū hadik	بغينا نجربو هدك

FOOD

... brochettes	qeṭban dyal ...	القطبان ديال ...
beef	bgrī	بكري
lamb	ghenemī	غنمي
liver	kebda	كبدة
heart	qelb	قلب
ground beef	kefta	كفتة

fava (broad) beans	lfūl	الفول
fried potatoes (chips)	frīt	بطاطا مقلية
peanuts	kawku	كاوكو
popcorn	lkelia	الكليا
rotisserie chicken	pūlī rūṭei	دجاج مشوي
salad	shalada	شلاضة
sandwich	kaskrūt	كسكروط
soup	ṣuba	صوبة

... eggs	beiḍ ...	بيض ...
scrambled	mterrba	مطربة
hard boiled	mslūqa	مصلوقة
fried	mqlīya	مقلية

TYPICAL DISHES

Moroccan cuisine is delicious, visually striking, and varied.
Here are some highlights of the country's rich culinary
tradition:

ṭāzhīn

A thick and richly spiced stew named for the round dish with
a cone-shaped cover in which it's prepared. Traditionally lamb
or mutton, ṭāzhīn can also be made of beef, fish or poultry.
Some of the most popular are lamb with prunes and onions,
chicken with lemon, chicken with almonds and hard boiled
eggs, and meatballs with eggs. The best are cooked over a
charcoal brazier. In homes, ṭāzhīn is eaten from the dish in
which it's cooked, placed in the centre of a low round table
and eaten by hand with bread.

kūskūs/seksū

The most popular meal in North Africa, kūskūs consists of
steamed semolina grain covered with a savoury meat and veg-
etable sauce. Kūskūs actually refers to the semolina grain, initially rolled by hand but now available dried and packaged.
Again, an almost infinite number of variations are available.
Two of the best are lamb with vegetables – most often including
carrots, turnips, cabbage, pumpkin and squash – and lamb with
raisins and onions. Customarily kūskūs is eaten by rolling it
into a ball and popping it in your mouth. This is really an
art and much more difficult than it looks – you might want
to give it a try, but keep a spoon handy!

besṭeila

This is the well-known Moroccan delicacy made of chicken
or pigeon, eggs, almonds, sugar and saffron, stuffed between
many layers of a crisp, paper-thin pastry. A must when visiting
the country, besṭeila can be specially ordered from many neighbourhood bakeries as well as the best Moroccan restaurants.

meshwī

Often found at weddings and other important occasions, meshwī is a complete lamb roasted and served in the centre of a table. Guests pull pieces of meat off with their hands and eat it with bread.

harīra

A thick, filling soup of tomatoes, lentils, chickpeas and meat seasoned with coriander and lemon. Traditionally used to break the fast during Ramadan, the Muslim month of fasting, harīra is now available at most Moroccan restaurants all year round.

atei benna'na

Mint tea in Morocco is not only a drink but a national institution, enjoyed in settings from Berber tents in the High Atlas to the King's Palace. Made with mint, green tea and sugar, each step in the preparation process appears carefully calculated, having been refined by countless repetitions. Expect many opportunities to experience the tea ritual first hand while staying in the country.

FOOD

SELF-CATERING

When purchasing food for a quick meal, the most convenient place to go is the neighbourhood grocery shop –hanūt. You'll be amazed at the variety of different items contained in such a small area. Typically, almost everything you'll want is behind the counter so here's a good chance to practise your Arabic. Don't expect an orderly queue during busy times – you might need to be assertive to get any service.

Where's a nearby grocer's shop?
 fīn kein shī hanūt dyal
 mwād lgheza'ya qrīb?

فين كاين شي حانوت ديال
المواد الغذائية قريب؟

How much is that?
 beshhal hadīk?

بشحال هدك؟

FOOD

Please give me a (half) kilo of cheese.

ʿaṭeinī wahed (neṣṣ) kīlū
dyal frumazh

عطيني واحد (نص) كيلو
الفورماجديال

Is there anything cheaper than that?

wash kein shī hazha rekheiṣa
ʿala hadīk?

واش كاينة شي حاجة رخيصة
علي هدك؟

Please give me a little bit of that.

ʿaṭeinī wahed shwīya min hadīk

عطيني واحد شوي من هدك

Add a little bit.

zīd shī shwīya

زيد شي شوي

Remove a little bit.

nqeṣ shī shwīya

نقص شي شوي

How much for ...?

bshhal ...?

بشحال . . . ؟

I don't want that one.

mabghītsh hadīk

مابغيتش هدك

Please give me that other one.

'afak ʿteinī hadīk lakhūra

عفاك عطيني هدك لخري

Please give me ...	ʿaṭeinī shī ... ʿafak	عطيني شي . . . عفاك
barley	shʿeir	شعير
bottled water	qerʿa dyal lma	قرعة ديال الماء
biscuits/sweets	helwat	حلوي

AT THE MARKET
Meat

beef	begrī	بكري
beef (ground)	kefta	كفتة
chicken	dzhazh	دجاج
heart	qelb	قلب
lamb	ghenmī	غنمي
liver	kebda	كبدة
meat	lhem	اللحم
pork	hellūf	حلوف
sausage	sūsis	صوصيص

Seafood

English	Transliteration	Arabic
anchovy	shṭun	شطون
cod	lamūrī	لاموري
eel	ṣemṭa	صمطة
lobster	lāngus	لانكوس
mussel	mūl	مول
sardine	serdīn	سردين
sea carp	qerb	قرب
shrimp	qeimrūn	قمرون
sole	ṣul	صول
squid	calamar	كالامار
tuna	ṭun	طون
whiting	merla	مرلة

FOOD

Vegetables

artichoke	qūq	قوق
beans (green)	lūbīya	الوبية
cabbage	krum	كروم
capsicum/pepper		
(green)	felfla	فلفلة
(red)	felfla hemra	فلفلة حمرة
carrot	khīzū	خيزو
cauliflower	shīflūr	شيفلور
celery	krafes	كرافس
coriander	qeṣbur	كزبور
cucumber	khyar	خيار

FOOD

eggplant	denzhal	دنجال
garlic	tūma	تومة
lettuce	kheṣṣ	خص
mushroom	feggīᶜ	فكيع
olive	zītūn	زيتون
onion	beṣla	بصلة
parsley	mᶜednūs	معدنوس
peas	zhelbana	جلبانة
potato	bṭāṭā	بطاطة
pumpkin/squash	gerᶜa hemra	كرعة حمرة
radish	fzhel	فجل
tomato	maṭeisha	مطيشة
turnip	left	لفت
vegetables	khuḍra	خضرة

Fruit

apple	teffah	تفاح
apricot	meshmash	مشماش
banana	bānān	بنان
cherries	hebb lemlūk	حب الملوك
date	tmer	تمر
fig	kermūs	كرموس
fruit	fakīya	فاكية
grapes	ᶜneb	عنب
lemon	hamed	حامض
orange	līmūn	ليمون
peach	khūkh	خوخ
pear	būᶜwīd	بوغويد
plum	berquq	برقوق
pomegranate	remman	رمان
prickly pear	kermūs lhendīya	كرموس الهندية
raisins	zbīb	زبيب
strawberries	tūt	توت
watermelon	dellah	دلاح

Dairy Products

butter	zebda	زبدة
buttermilk	lben	لبن
cheese	frumazh	فرماج
ice cream	laglas	لكلاس
milk	hlib	حليب
yogurt	danūn	دانون

FOOD

Spices & Condiments

cinnamon	qerfa	قرفة
clove	qrunfel	قرونفل
cumin	kamūn	كمون
ginger	sken zhbir	سكن جبير
hot pepper	felfla harra	فلفلة حارة
hot sauce	hrūr	حرور
jam	kunfitūr	كونفيتير
mustard	mūtard	موتارد
oil	zīt	زيت
olive oil	zīt lᶜūd	زيت العود
paprika	felfla hamra	فلفلة حمرة
pepper	lebzār	البزار
salt	melha	ملحة
sugar	sūkkar	سكر
saffron	zaᶜfran	زعفران
sesame	zhenzhlan	جنجلان

DRINKS

beer	bīra	بيرة
black tea	atei nnegru	اتاي نكرو
cold water	lma berd	الماء بارد
hot water	lma skhūn	الماء سخن
juice	ʿāṣeir	عصير
milk	hlīb	حليب
mint tea	atei bennaʿnaʿ	اتاي بنعنع
soft drink	munāḍa	مونادة
wine	shrab	شراب
coffee ...	qehwa ...	قهوة ...
black	kehla	كحلة
with milk	belhlīb	بالحليب
with a little bit of milk	mherresa	محرسة

FOOD

IN THE COUNTRY

CAMPING

Where's the campsite?
fīn kein lmukheyyem?
فين كاين المخيم؟

Is there a site available?
wash keina shī blāṣā khawīya?
واش كاينة شي بلاصة خاوية؟

Is it OK for us to camp here?
wesh makein mūshkil īla
kheyyemna henna?
واش ما كين مشكل الي
خيمنا هنا؟

Is there a shower?
wash kein shī ḍūzh?
واش كاين شي دوش؟

Where can I hire a tent?
fīn yemkenlī nkrī shīgīṭūn?
فين يمكن لي نكري شي كطون؟

backpack	ṣakkaḍō	صاك اضو
firewood	hteb	حطب
gas cartridge	bōṭa dyal lgaz	بوطة ديال الكاز
hammer	mterqa	مترقة
knife	mūs	موس
rope	qenba	قنبة
sleeping bag	ṣak dyal kūsazh	صاك د كوساج
stove	furnu	فورنو
tent	gīṭūn	كيطون
torch/flash light	pīl	بيل

HIKING

Where can I find information about hiking in the area?

fin yemken lī nelga shī mᶜalūmat bash ndōrū f had nahīya?

فين يمكن لي لقي شي معلومات باشنضورو ف هل النحية؟

I want to talk with someone who knows this area.

bghīt ntkellem mᶜa shī wahed llī keiᶜarf had nahīya

بغيت نتكلم مع شي واحد لي تيعرف هد الناحية

Where can I find a guide?

fīn yemkenlī nelga shī gīd?

فين يمكن لي نلقي شي كيد؟

How long is the hike?

shhal dyal lweqt kein f
had ḍḍōra?

شحال ديال الوقت كاين ف هد ضورة؟

Is the trail well marked?

wash lᶜalama beina?

واش العلامة باينة؟

Which is the shortest route?

'ashmen ṭrīq qrība?

اش من طريق قريبة؟

Is the trail open all year?

wash ṭrīq mehūla lᶜam kūlū?

واش طريق محلولة العام كولو؟

Is the trail scenic?

wash ṭrīq fīha shī menḍer?

واش طريق فيها شي مناظر؟

Where can I buy supplies?

fīn yemkenlī neshrī ᶜwīn?

فين يمكن لي نشري العوين؟

On the path

Where have you come from?

mnīn zhītī?

منين جيتي؟

How long did it take you?

shhal dyal weqt keikheṣṣek?

شحال ديال الوقت كيخصك؟

Does this path go to ...?

wash had ṭrīq ghadīya l ...?

واش هد طريق غادية ل . . . ؟

altitude	ᶜlu	العلو
binoculars	shwafat	شوفات
cliff	ṣkher	صخر
climb (v)	ṭleᶜ	طلع
compass	bawṣala	بوصلة
downhill	ḥabeṭ	هابط
forest	ghaba	غابة
guide	gīd	كيد
hike (n)	ḍōwira	ضورة
itinerary	ṭrīq	طريق
ledge	hashīya	الحاشية
map	kharīṭa	خريطة
mountain	zhbel	جبل
pass	triyqa	طريقة
peak	raṣ	راس
steep	qaseḥ	قاصح
uphill	ṭaleᶜ	طالع
valley	sehl	سهل
view	menḍer	منظر
village	duwwar	دوار
walk (v)	temsha ᶜla rezhlīn	تمش علا الرجلين

IN THE COUNTRY

I'm lost.
tweḍḍert
تضرت

Where can we spend the night?
fīn yemken līna nbatū had līla?
فين يمكن لنا نباتو هد الليلة؟

Can I leave some things here?
wash neqder nkhellī shī
hawezh hna?
واش نقدر نخلي شي حاجة هنا؟

AT THE BEACH

Is there a beach near here?
  wash kein shī sheṭṭ qrīb l hna?

واش كاين شي شاط قريب لهنا؟

Can we swim here?
  wash nqedrū n'ūmū hna?

واش نقدرو نعومو هنا؟

Is it safe to swim?
  wash mashi khaṭar l 'uman?

واش ماشي خطر العومان؟

coast	muhīt	محيط
fishing	sīyada	صيادة
rock	hzher	حجر
sand	remla	رملة
sea	bher	بحر
sunblock	krīm dyal shems	كريم ديال الشمس
sunglasses	ndaḍer dyal shems	الشمس نضاضر ديال
surfing	sōrf	سورف
swimming	'ūman	العومان
towel	fōṭa	فوطة
waves	muzhat	موجات

IN THE COUNTRY

WEATHER

How's the weather there?
  kee dayer lzhū dyal temma?

كي داير الجو ديال تما؟

Is it ... there?	wash kein ... temma?	واش كاين تما . . . ؟
hot	ṣṣehd	صهد
cold	lberd	البرد
cloudy	ḍḍbāba	ضباب

humid	rruṭuba	الرطوبة
raining	shṭa	الشتاء
snowing	ttelzh	الثلج
windy	rrīḥ	الريح

What's the temperature today?

shḥal feddārāzhat dyal
harara lyūm?

شحال فدراجات ديال الحرارة اليوم؟

What's the weather going to be like today?

kīfash ghādī īkūn lzhūw lyūm?

كفاش غادي يكون الجو اليوم؟

drought	zhafaf	الجفاف
dry	nashef	ناشف
flood	fayaḍan	الفيضان
lightning	breq	البرق
mud	ghīs	الغيس
rain	shṭa	الشتاء
rainbow	qwas quzah	قوس قز
shade	ḍḍel	ضل
sky	sma	سماء
storm	ʿaṣifa	عاصفة
sun	shems	شمس
thunder	rʿad	رعد
weather	zhū	جو
wind	rīḥ	ريح

SEASONS

winter	shtwa	شتوا
spring	rbīᶜ	ربيع
summer	ṣeif	صيف
autumn/fall	khrīf	خريف

GEOGRAPHICAL TERMS

beach	laplāzh	شاطيء
bridge	qenṭra	قنطرة
cave	lakab	لكاب
cliff	skher	صخر
countryside	badīya	بادية
desert	ṣehra	صحراء
earthquake	zelzal	زلزال
farm	firma	فيرمة
forest	ghaba	غابة
harbor	mersa	مرسي
hill	haḍaba	هضبة
island	zhazīra	جزيرة
lake	ḍaya	ضاية
moon	qamar	قمر
mountain	zhbel	جبل
ocean	bhar	بحر
river	wad	واد

road	ṭraiq	طريق
rock	hezhra	حجرة
sand	remla	رملة
sun	shems	شمس
star	nzhma	نجمة
valley	wad	واد
waterfall	shellalat	شلالات

ANIMALS & INSECTS

bee	nehla	نحلة
bird	ṭeir	طير
butterfly	fertaṭō	فرطاطو
camel	zhmel	جمل
cat	meshsh	مش
chicken	dzhazha	دجاجة
cockroach	ṣerraq zzīt	سراق زيت
cow	begra	بكرة
deer	kurkdan	كركدان
dog	kelb	كلب
donkey	hmar	حمار
fish	hūta	حوتة
fly	debbana	دبانة
goat	meᶜza	معزة
horse	ᶜawd	العاود
monkey	qerd	قرد
mosquito	sniwala	سنيولة
mule	beghl	بغل
pig	hellūf	حلوف
rabbit	qnīya	قنية
rooster	ferrūzh	فروج
sheep	hawlī	حاولي
snail	babbūsh	بابوش
snake	hensh	حنش

spider	rtīla	رتيلة
squirrel	sebseb	سبسب
wild animal	Hayawan	حيوان

FLORA & AGRICULTURE

agriculture	felaha	فلاحة
bush	ghaba	غابة
crops	ṣaba	صبة
flower	werda	وردة
forest	ghaba	غابة
field	feddan	فدان
grass	rbīᶜ	ربيع
harvest (v)	hṣed	حصد
irrigation	sqa	سقا
leaf	werqa	ورقة
olive tree	shezhra dyal zzītūn	الزيتون شجرة ديال
plant	nebet	نبت
rose	werda	وردة
tree	shezhra	شجرة

IN THE COUNTRY

HEALTH

Anyone unfortunate enough to become ill will have no trouble finding the medicine they need at any chemist in a major city. Those who need a doctor have the choice of nationally funded health services or private doctors and clinics. You'll find the French language invaluable when dealing with the Moroccan medical system, as all doctors are educated in French and use it to write prescriptions and instructions for taking medicine.

Where's a/the ...?	fīn kein ...?	...كاين؟ فين
doctor	shī ṭbīb	شي طبيب
hospital	ṣṣebīṭār	صبيطار
chemist	lfārmasyan	الفرماسيان
dentist	shī ṭbīb dyal ssnan	طبيب ديال سنان

I'm sick.
  ana mrīḍ

انا مريض

My friend is sick.
  saḥbī mrīḍ

صاحبي مريض

I need a doctor whospeaks English.
  bghīt shī ṭbīb llī keihder
  nneglizīya

بغيت واحد طبيب اللي
كيحضر انكليزية

Can the doctor come here?
  wash ṭṭbīb iqder īzhī l hna?

واش اقدر طبيب اجي لهنا؟

Can the doctor come with me?
  wash ṭṭbīb iqder īzhī mʿaya?

واش طبيب يقدر اجي معي؟

AILMENTS

I have a headache.

keiḍerrnī rāṣī

كايضرني راسي

I have a cold.

ana mrewweh

انا مروح

THE DOCTOR MAY SAY ...

What happened?

weqaʿ?

اش وقع؟

Do you feel any pain?

wash kathess beluwzhʿ?

واش كتحس ب لوجع؟

Where does it hurt?

fīn keiḍerrek?

فين كيضرك؟

Do you have a temperature?

wash fīk skhana?

واش فيك سخانة؟

How long have you been like this?

shhal hadī ū 'nta hakka?

شحال هد انت حق؟

Is this the first time you've had this?

wash hadī 'uwwela merra
llī 'andek hadshī?

واش هيد اول مرة عندك
هد شي؟

Are you taking any medication?

wash katakhōd shī dwa?

واش كتاخذ شي دوي؟

Do you smoke?

wash katkmī?

واش كتكمي؟

Do you drink?

wash katshreb?

واش كتشرب؟

Are you allergic to anything?

wash 'andek lhasasīya
dyal shī hazha?

واش عندك الحساسية
ديال شي حاجة؟

Are you pregnant?

wash 'ntī hamla?

واش انتي حاملة؟

I have a fever.
  fīya skhana   فيي سخانة

I have diarrhoea.
  kershī zharīya   كرشي جارية

I feel nauseous.
  kanhess mekhūm   كنحس مكهوم

I'm constipated.
  fīya lqabeṭ   فيي القبط

I've been vomiting.
  kanteqqīya   كنتقيا

I can't sleep.
  manqdersh nnᶜes   ماقدرش نعس

I feel ...	kanhess ...	كنحس ...
dizzy	dayekh	دايخ
shivery	tbūrīsha	تبوريشة
weak	merkhī	مرخي

I have (a/an) ...	ᶜendi	عندي ...
allergy	lhasasīya	الحساسية
anaemia	ḍuᶜf feddem	ضعف في الدم
asthma	digga	ديقة
blister	mnebbel	منبل
bites	qrīṣ	قريص
burn	mehrōq	محروق
cancer	kunṣir	كنسير
cold	lberd	البرد
cough	khba	كحبة
cut	zherha	جرحة
diabetes	merḍ ṣōkkar	مرض السكر
epilepsy	lrīyah	لرياح
heart condition	merḍ lqelb	مرض القلب
high blood pressure	laṭṭensīyu	لطنسيون
influenza	menzla	منزلة

infection	zhra	الجرحة
itch	hekka	الحكة
lice	gmel	الكمل
migrain	shqīqa	شقيقة
pain	lyzheᶜ	لوجع
rash	hbūb	حبوب
sore throat	hlaqem	حلاقم
stomach ache	lūzheᶜ f lmᶜda	لوجع ف المعدة
sunburn	lhrīq dyal shshemsh	لحرق ديال الشمس
tooth ache	luzheᶜ dyal ssnan	لوجع ديال لسنان
travel sickness	merda dyal ssafar	مرضة ديال السفر
worms	ddud	دود

Useful Words & Phrases

It hurts here.

    keiḍernī henna   كيوجعني هنا

I feel better/worse.

    kanhess hsen/kfes   كنحس احسن / كفيس

This is my usual medicine.

    hada hūwa ddwa dyal dīma   هد هو دوي ديالي ديما

I've been vaccinated.

    dert zhelba   درت جلبة

I don't want a blood transfusion.

    mabghīts ndīr ddemm   ما بغيتش ندير دم

Please give me the bill.

    ᶜafak ᶜṭainī lhsab   عفاك عطيني الحساب

HEALTH

My ... hurts.	katḍerrnī ...	... كتضرني
back	ḍehrī	ضهري
hand	yeddī	يدي
leg/foot	rezhlī	رجلي

Is it broken?	wash mherresa?	واش مهرسة؟
Is it sprained?	wash mfdūˤ?	واش مفدوع؟
I'm bleeding.	kansīl beddem	كنسيل بدم

accident	ksīda	كسيدا
addiction	blīya	بلية
AIDS	sīda	سيدا
bandage	bunda	بندة
blood group	nuwˤ dyal ddem	النوع ديال الدم
blood pressure	laṭṭensīyu	لطانسيون
blood test	thlīl dyal ddem	تحليل ديال الدم
burn	herqa	حرقة
contagious	keitˤada	كيتعد
cream/ointment	pumada	بوماد
dangerous	khāṭār	خطر
infected	mˤeffen	معفن
injection	shūka	شوكة
laboratory	mukhtabar	مختبر
medicine	ddawa	دوي
nurse	fermlīya	فرملية
pain	hrīq/wzheˤ	حريق/وجع
patient	lmrīḍ.	المريض
poison	semm	سم
sanitary	shhī	صحي
swell (v)	nfekh	نفخ
syringe	huqna	حقنة
test (laboratory)	thlīl	تحليل
urine	bōl	بول
vitamin	vītamīn	فينامين

WOMEN'S HEALTH

Can I see a female doctor?
wash neqder nshūf shī ṭbība
dyal lᶜyalet?

واش نقدر نشوف طبيبة
ديال العيلات؟

I prefer a woman.
kanfḍel lmra

كنفضل امراة

I'm pregnant.
ana hamla

انا حاملة

I'd like to take a pregnancy test.
bghīt nuwwez thlīl dyal lhmel

بغيت ندوز تحليلات علي الحمل

I haven't had my period for ... weeks.
mahanīsh hak ... shahr ldām

محانيش... حق شهر الدم

contraception	ḍed lhmal	منع الحمل
diaphragm	dyafram	ديافراكم
menstruation	heq shher	حق الشهر

SPECIAL HEALTH NEEDS

I'm ...	ana ...	انا ...
anaemic	faqer f ddemm	فقر ف الدم
asthmatic	fīya ddīga	في ديقة
diabetic	fīya merḍ ssukkar	في مرض السكر

I've got high/low blood pressure.
ᶜandī lattensiyu taleᶜ/nazel

عندي لطنسيون طالع/نازل

I have a weak heart.
ᶜandī lqelb dᶜīf

عندي القلب ضعيف

HEALTH

I take regular medication.

    kandawem dwa   كنداوم دوي

I'm on a special diet.

    kan dīr rrīzhīm   دایر رجیم

I have my own syringe.

    ʿandī shūka dyalī   عندي شوكة ديالي

I'm allergic to ...	ʿandī lhsasīya mʿa ...	... عندي الحساسية مع
bees	nhel	نحل
dairy products	makla llī fīha lhlīb	الحليب مكلة اللي فيها
penicillin	lbīnselīn	بنسلين
this	hadī	هد

PARTS OF THE BODY

arm	dreʿ	درع
back	dher	ضهر
blood	demm	دم
bone	ʿdem	عضم
chest	sder	صدر
ear	wden	ودن
eye	ʿīn	عین
face	wzheh	وجه
finger	sbeʿ	صبع
foot	rzhel	رجل
hair	shʿar	شعار
hand	yedd	ید
head	rāṣ	راس
heart	qelb	قلب
leg	rzhel	رجل
liver	kebda	كبد
lung	reyya	رية
mouth	fūmm	فوم
shoulder	ktef	كتف

HEALTH

skin	zheld	جلد
teeth	snan	سنان
throat	hleq	الحلق
toe	ṣbeʿ	صبع
tongue	lsan	لسان

AT THE CHEMIST

Do you have medicine for (a) ...?	wash ʿandek ddwa dyal ...?	واش عندك دوي ديال ... ؟
cold	rrewwah	رواح
cough	lkehha	الكحة
diarrhoea	sshal	سهال
headache	rraṣ	الراس
sore throat	lhlaqem	الحلقم
stomachache	wazheʿ lmʿda	وجع المعدة

Do I need a prescription?
wash kheṣṣnī shī werqa
dyal ṭṭbīb?
واش خصني شي ورقة ديال الطبيب؟

How many should I take each time?
sHal men waHda ghadī nakūl
kūl merra?
شحال من واحدة غادي ناكل كل مرة؟

How many times per day?
shhal men merra fennhar?
شحال من مرة ف النهار؟

antibiotics	ʾantībīyutīk	اننتيبيوتيك
aspirin	asperīn	اسبرين
bandage	banda	باندا
condoms	kapūt	كبوط
contraceptives	dwa dyal lhmel	دوي ضد الحمل
gauze	faṣma	فاصمة
pain killers	muhdden	مهدن
sleeping pills	dwa dyal nnʿas	دوي ديال النعس

HEALTH

AT THE DENTIST

I have a toothache.
    fīya ddersa
في ضرسة

I've got a cavity.
    fīya ssūsa
في صوسة

I've lost a filling.
    taht līya l'mara dyal ddersa
طاحت لي العمر ديال ضرسة

I've broken a tooth.
    therresat līya ssenna
تهرست لي السنة

My gums hurt.
    keyderrnī lhem dyal ssnan
كيضريني لحم ديال سنان

Don't extract it!
    matgle'hash!
ماتكلعهاش!

Give me an anaesthetic!
    dīr līya lbenzh!
در لي البنج!

AT THE OPTOMETRIST

I want my eyes tested.
    bhīt ndewwez 'ala 'īnī
بغيت ندوز علي عيني

I'm long/short sighted.
    makanshūfsh b'aīd/qrīb
ما كنشوفش بعيد / قريب

Please fix my glasses.
    'afak şoweb nndader dyalī
عفاك صوب لي نضاضر ديالي

I'd like new glasses.
    bghīt ndader zhdad
بغيت نضاضر جداد

I'd like new contact lenses.
    bghīt l'adadsat dyal l'inìn zhdad
بغيت عدسات ديال العنين جداد

HEALTH

I'd like contact lens solution.
    bghīt lmadda llī keighslū bīha
    lᶜadadsat dyal lᶜinīn

العدسات للعنين بغيت المادة
اللي كيغسلو بها

DISABLED TRAVELLERS

I'm ...	ana ...	... انا
disabled/handicapped	muᶜewweq	معوق
blind	ᶜma	عمي
deaf	smek	سمك

I need assistance.

bhīt llī īwqef mᶜya   بغيت لي يوقف معي

Do you have services for disabled people?

wesh keina shī meslaha mekhtaṣṣa   واش كاين شي مصلحة مختصة

belmuᶜewweqīn?   بالمعوقين؟

Is there wheelchair access?

wesh keina shī kerrusa dyal   واش كاين شي كروسة

lmuᶜewwaqīn?   ديال المعوقين؟

Speak louder please.

tkellem bezhzhhed ᶜafak   تكلم ب جهد عفاك

Speak more slowly please.

tkellem beshwīya ᶜafak   تكلم ب شوية عفاك

DID YOU KNOW ...   Moroccans can be very sensitive about their Royal Family - the King claims direct descent from the Prophet, and criticism of him may be viewed as blasphemous.

SPECIFIC NEEDS

Will there be a guide to explain things?
    wesh kein shī murshed?
    واش كاين شي مرشد؟

I'm hard of hearing.
    ʿandī ssmeʿ tqīl
    عندي سمع تقيل

I have a hearing aid.
    ʿandī lapparay dyal ssmeʿ
    عندي لبراي ديال سمع

Are guide dogs permitted?
    wesh lkelb llī kaygiyyid lʿma   واش الكلب يلي كيكيد العمي مسموح
    mesmuh līh īdkhel?   ليه ادخل؟

TRAVELLING WITH A FAMILY

I'm travelling with my family.
    ana mṣafer mʿa lʿaīla dyalī
    انا مسافر مع العايلة ديالي

Are there facilities for babies?
    wesh kein tshīlat dyal   واش كاين تسهيلات ديال دراري
    ddrarī ṣghar?   صغار؟

Are there going to be other families?
    wesh ghadī īkūnū lʿaʾīlat   واش غادي يكونو العاءلات اخرين؟
    akhrin?

Do you have a baby-sitting service?
    wesh kein ʿandkum dar lhaḍana?   واش كاين عندكم دار لحضانة؟

Where can I find an English-speaking
baby-sitter?

    fīn yemken llī nelga wahed
    lmurabbīya dyal ddrarī ṣṣghar
    llī keitkellem benneg1īzīya?

فين يمكن لي نلقي واحد المربية
ديال دراري صغار لي
كيتكلم بانكليزية؟

Can you put an extra bed in the room?

    wesh teqder ddīr wahed ssrīr
    dyal drarī ṣghar zayd felbīt?

واش تقدر تدير واحد سرير ديال
دراري صغار زايد ف البيت؟

I need a car with a child seat.

    bghīt wahed ṭṭōmōbīl belkōrsī
    dyal drarī ṣghar

بغيت واحد طوموبيل بالكرسي
ديال دراري صغار

Is it suitable for children?

    wesh mnaseb l drarī ṣghar?

واش مناسب لدراري صغار؟

Body Language

Public displays of affection are common between friends of the
same sex, but frowned on between couples, even when married. Handshakes, kisses and hugs are all common greetings.

Are there any activities for children?
 wesh kein shī tanshīṭ dyal
 drarī ṣghar?

واش كاين شي تنشيط ديال
دراري صغار؟

Is there a family discount?
 wesh ken shī tekhfiṭ bennsiba
 lᶜa'īla?

واش كاين شي تخفيض بالنسبة
للعائلة؟

Are children allowed?
 wesh mesmuh l drarī?

واش مسموح للدراري؟

Is there a playground nearby?
 wesh kein shī ssaha dyal llᶜeb qrība?

كاين شي الساحة ديال اللعب
واش قريبة؟

TIMES, DATES & FESTIVALS

TELLING THE TIME

Telling the time in Morocco is fairly straightforward. The abbreviations 'am'and 'pm' are expressed in whole words, for example, '8 am' is literally '8 in the morning', ttmenya feṣṣbah; '2 pm' is '2 in the afternoon', zhzhūzh fel'shīya; and '8 pm' is '8 at night', ttmenya fellīl

Hours

It's ... o'clock	hadī ...	... هادي
1	lewhda	الوحدة
2	zhzhūzh	جوج
3	ttlata	تلاتة
4	rreb"a	اربعة
5	lkhamsa	خمسة
6	ssetta	ستة
7	sseb"a	سبعة
8	ttmenya	تمنية
9	tts'ūd	تسعود
10	l'ashra	عشرة
11	lhdash	حضاش
12	ṭṭnash	طناش
morning	feṣṣbah	صباح
afternoon	fel'shīya	عشية
night	fellīl	ليلا
hour	sa'a	ساعة
two hours	sa'atein	ساعتين
more than two hours	swaye'	سوية

What time is it?	shal fessaᶜa?	شحال فالساعة؟
It's three exactly.	hadī ttlata nīshan	هادي تلاتة نيشان
It's about four.	hadī rrebᶜa teqrīben	هادي ربعة تقريبا

Minutes

Minutes are expressed after the hour and divided into groups of
five. The literal translation gives an idea of how the system works.

It's ...	hadī ...	... هادي
1.05 (one and one five minute period)	lewhda ūqṣem	الواحدة وقسم
1.10 (one and two five minute periods)	lewhda ūqeṣmein	الواحدة و قسمين
1.15 (one and 1/4)	lewhda ūrbâᶜ	الواحدة وربع
1.20 (one and 1/3)	lewhda ūtūlūt	الواحدة و تلت
1.25 (one and 25)	lewhda ūkhamsa ūᶜshrīn	الواحدة و خمسة و عشرين
1.30 (one and 1/2)	lewheda ūneṣṣ	الواحدة و نص
1.35 (two less 25)	zhzhūzh qell khamsa ūᶜshrīn	جوج قل خمسة و عشرين
1.40 (two less 1/3)	zhzhūzh qell tūlūt	جوج قل تلت
1.45 (two less 1/4)	zhzhūzh llarūb	جوج الا ربع
1.50 (two less two five minute periods)	zhzhūzh qell qeṣmein	جوج قل قسمين
1.55 (two less one five minute period)	zhzhūzh qell qṣem	جوج قل قسم

minute	dqīqa	دقيقة
minutes	dqayeq	دقايق
second	tanīya	ثانية
seconds	tanīyat	ثانيات
five minutes	qsem	قسم
ten minutes	qeṣmein	قسمين

TIMES, DATES & FESTIVALS

DAYS

Sunday	nhar lhedd	نهار الحد
Monday	nhar letnīn	نهار لتنين
Tuesday	nhar ttlat	نهار تلات
Wednesday	nhar larbᶜ	نهار لاربع
Thursday	nhar lekhmīs	نهار لخميس
Friday	nhar zhzhemᶜa	نهار جمع
Saturday	nhar ssebt	نهار سبت

| What day is it today? | shnū lyūm? | شنو ليوم؟ |

day	nhar	نهار
two days	yūmein	يومين
three days	teltīyam	تلتيام
this week	had l'ūsbūᶜ/ssīmana	هدا الاسبوع / سيمانا
two weeks	zhūzhdel'asabīᶜ/ dessīmanat	جوج دل اسابيع / دسيمانات

MONTHS

Morocco operates on two calendar systems – the standard Western, or Gregorian system, and the Muslim calendar. In general, all business and government affairs are conducted by the Western calendar and this is the one you'll need to know.

The Muslim calendar, used in Morocco mainly for religious holidays, consists of a 354 day year divided into 12 lunar months. A day is added to the last month 11 times in every 30 years, so that in a century the Muslim calendar differs from the Gregorian calendar by just over two years. The first day of the first year corresponds to 15 July 622 AD, the year in which Mohammed and his followers migrated from Mecca to Medina.

January	zhanvīyeh	جنفيه
February	fevrīyeh	فڤريه
March	mars	مارس
April	abrīl	ابريل
May	mayyū	مايو
June	yūnyū	يونيو
July	yūlyūz	يوليوز
August	ghūsht	غشت
September	sebtamber	سبتمبر
October	'ūktūber	اكتوبر
November	nūvamber	نفمبر
December	dīsamber	دسمبر
a month	shher	شهر
two months	shehrein	شهرين
three months	telt shhūr	تلت شهور
a year	ʿam	عام
two years	ʿamein	عامين
three years	telt snīn	تلت سنين

TIMES, DATES & FESTIVALS

PRESENT

now	daba	دابا
today	lyūm	ليوم
this month	had shshhar	هدا الشهر
this year	had l^cam	هدا العام

PAST

yesterday	lbareh	لبارح
day before yesterday	wellbareh	وللبارح
yesterday morning	lbareh fessbah	لبارح ف لصباح
last week	l'ūsbū^c llī fat	الاسبوع الي فات
last month	shshhar llī fat	الشهر الي فات
last year	l^cam llī fat	العام الي فات

FUTURE

an hour from now	men daba wahed ssa^ca	من دابا واحد الساعة
tomorrow	ghedda	غدا
tomorrow afternoon	ghedda fel^cshīya	غدا ف العشية

Psst ...

People may try to get your attention by making a hissing sound. It's used by motorists as a warning to get out of the way, and also as the equivalent of a wolf whistle.

day after tomorrow	bᶜd ghedda	بعد غدا
next week	l'ūsbūᶜ llī zhei	الاسبوع الي جاي
a week from today	bhal lyūm	بحال ليوم
next month	shshhar llī zhei	الشهر الي جاي
next year	lᶜam llī zhei	العام الي جاي

around	zhwayeh	جوايح
on time	felweqt	فالوقت
early	bekrī	بكري
late	mᶜettel	معطل
hurry up	serbī	سربي
early in the morning	feṣṣbāh bekrī	ف صباح بكري
past	lmāḍei	الماضين
present	lhāḍer	الحاضر
future	lmüsteqbal	المستقبل

FESTIVALS

Morocco has a number of religious and government holidays representing the country's rich historical and cultural traditions. Since the Muslim holidays are based on the Islamic calender, the date of their occurence will vary from year to year.

Ramadan
رمضان

This is the Islamic month of fasting. From sunrise to sunset each day, Muslims refrain from eating, drinking, smoking and other worldly pleasures unless they're ill, pregnant, nursing, travelling, below the age of puberty or otherwise unable. Obviously this causes major disruptions in the pattern of daily life. Businesses usually open mid-morning and close around 4 pm. During the day, activity slows down considerably only to increase in the evening as the cafes and streets remain full until after midnight. While Ramadan can present problems for travellers, in many ways it's an exciting time to be in the country. The religious significance combined with the festive atmosphere in the evenings and many special foods make it a favourite time of year for many Moroccans.

One word of advice during Ramadan, be sensitive to those who are fasting during the day. When possible try not to eat, drink or smoke in public and make an effort to dress conservatively.

fasting	ssīyam	الصيام
Are you fasting?	wash 'nta ṣeim?	واش انت صايم ؟
Where are you going to break the fast?	fīn ghadī tefṭer?	فين غادي تفطر؟

Aid el kbir   ʕīd lkbīr   عيد الكبير
Probably the most important religious holiday of the year, Aid el kbir is when Muslims celebrate Abraham's willingness to sacrifice his son. Most families buy a sheep to sacrifice after morning prayers and then eat throughout the day.

Throne day   ʕīd lʕarsh   عيد العرش
This, the most significant government holiday, celebrates King Hassan II's ascension to the throne. Festivities include parades and traditional concerts throughout the country.

TIMES, DATES & FESTIVALS

Where's the parade?
    fin ghadī īkūn l'istiʿrad?

فين غادي يكون الاستعراض؟

When will the parade begin?
    'imta ghadī ībda l'istiʿrad?

امتي غادي يبدآ الاستعراض؟

Will there be a concert today?
    wash ghadi īkūn sh ṭṭarab lyum?

واش غادي يكون الطرب اليوم؟

NUMBERS & AMOUNTS

Due to its colonisation by France, Morocco uses standard Western numerical symbols rather than those normally associated with Arab countries.

CARDINAL NUMBERS

1	wahed	واحد
2	zhūzh	جوج
3	tlata	تلاتة
4	reb^ca	ربعة
5	khamsa	خمسة
6	setta	ستة
7	seb^ca	سبعة
8	tmenya	تمنية
9	tes^cūd	تسعود
10	^cashra	عشرة

'uh-oh'

The glottal stop in Moroccan Arabic is also heard in English - it's the sound made between the vowels in 'uh-oh'

NUMBERS & AMOUNTS

11	hḍāsh	حضاش
12	ṭnāsh	طناش
13	telṭāsh	تلطاش
14	rbaᶜṭāsh	ربعطاش
15	khamsṭāsh	خمسطاش
16	seṭṭāsh	سطاش
17	sbeᶜṭāsh	سبعطاش
18	tmenṭāsh	تمنطاش
19	tseᶜṭāsh	تسعطاش
20	ᶜashrīn	عشرين
21	wahed ū ᶜashrīn	واحد و عشرين
22	tnein ū ᶜashrīn	تنين و عشرين
23	tlata ū ᶜashren	تلاتة و عشرين
30	tlatīn	تلاتين
40	rebᶜīn	ربعين
50	khamsīn	خمسين
60	settīn	ستين
70	sebᶜīn	سبعين
80	tmanīn	تمانين
90	tesᶜīn	تسعين
100	mya	مية
200	myatein	ميتين
300	teltmya	تلات مية
400	rbaᶜmya	ربع مية
500	khemsmya	خمس مية
600	settemya	ست مية
700	sbeᶜmya	سبع مية
800	temnemya	تمن مية
900	tseᶜmya	تسع مية
1000	alf	الف
2000	alfein	الفين
3000	telt alaf	تلت الاف
10,000	ᶜashra alaf	عشرة الاف
100,000	meyat alf	مية الف

one million	melyūn	مليون
two million	zhūzh delmlein	جوج د الملايين
one billion	melyar	مليار

Multiples

To form multiples, simply string the appropriate numbers
together, separating them with ū.

225	myatein ūkhamsa ū'shrīn	ميتين و خمسة و عشرين
1989	alf ūtse'meyya	الف و تسع مية و
	ūts'ūd ūtmanīn	تسعود و ثمانين

ORDINAL NUMBERS

first	lūwwel	الاول
second	tanī	تاني
third	talet	تالت
fourth	rabe'	رابع
fifth	khames	خامس
sixth	sades	سادس
seventh	sabe'	سابع
eighth	tamen	تامن
ninth	tase'	تاسع
tenth	'asher	عاشر

NUMBERS & AMOUNTS

the first bus	lkar llūwwel	الكار الاول
the third street	zzenqa ttalta	الزنقة تالتة

to count	hseb	حسب
equal	bhal bhal	بحال بحال
half	neṣṣ	نص
a quarter	rbeᶜ	ربع
per cent	felmya	فلمية

NUMBERS & AMOUNTS

The Berber language is spoken throughout North Africa, with speakers concentrated in Morocco and Algeria. An ancient people with a reputation as fierce warriors, the Berbers have notoriously resisted outside control, managing to maintain their language and cultural practices under Roman, Vandal and Arab rule. Today the Berber people of Morocco largely inhabit mountain regions and parts of the desert. There are three main ethnic groups, which can be loosely identified by dialect.

In the north, centred on the Rif, the locals speak a dialect which has been called Riffian and is spoken as far south as Figuig on the Algerian frontier. The dialect that predominates in the Middle and High Atlas and the valleys leading into the Sahara goes by various names, including Braber or Amazigh.

More settled tribes of the High Atlas, Anti-Atlas, Souss Valley and south-western oases generally speak Tashelhit or Chleuh. The following phrases are a selection from the Tashelhit dialect, the one visitors are likely to find most useful.

Berber may be written in Arabic or Roman script, although the Berbers have traditionally maintained an oral culture transmitted from generation to generation through storytelling and song.

You Should Know

Is there ...?	ees eela ...?
Do you have ...?	ees daroon ...?
I want ...	reeh ...
Give me ...	feeyee ...
How much is it?	minshk aysker?
food	teeremt
water	amen
mule	aserdon
somewhere to sleep	kra lblast mahengwen
big/small	mqorn/eemzee
a lot/little	bzef/eemeek
too expensive	nuqs emeek
no good	oor eefulkeemqorn/ eemzee
today	zig sbah
tomorrow	ghasad
yesterday	eegdam

MEETING PEOPLE

Hello.	la bes darik/darim (m/f)
Hello (in response).	la bes
Goodbye.	akayaoon arbee
Please.	barakalaufik
Thank you.	barakalaufik
Yes.	eyeh
No.	oho

BERBER

Excuse me.	semhee
How are you?	meneek antgeet?
Fine, thank you.	la bes, lhamdulah
Good.	eefulkee/eeshwa
Bad.	khaib
See you later.	akrawes dah inshallah

GETTING AROUND

I want to go to ...	reeh ...
Where is (the) ...?	mani heela ...?
mountain	adrar
pass	tizee
river	aseet
village	doorwar
Is it far/close?	ees yagoog/eeqareb?
straight	neeshan
to the right	fofaseenik
to the left	fozelmad

NUMBERS

1	yen	6	sddes
2	seen	7	sa
3	krad	8	tem
4	koz	9	tza
5	smoos	10	mrawet

BERBER

11	yen d mrawet
12	seen d mrawet
20	ashreent
21	ashreent d yen d mrawet
22	ashreent d seen d mrawet
30	ashreent d mrawet
40	snet id ashreent
50	snet id ashreent d mrawet
100	smoost id ashreent/meeya

The most commonly spoken European language in Morocco is French, a legacy of Morocco's time as a French protectorate from 1912 until independence was regained in 1956. If the thought of getting your tongue around Arabic is too much, it would be a good investment to learn some French.

The following words and phrases should help you communicate in French on a basic level:

PRONUNCIATION

French pronunciation can be difficult for an English speaker but if you remember a few basic rules, you won't have any trouble making yourself understood.

Vowels

a   as in the 'u' in 'cup'
e   barely pronounced, as the 'e' in 'open'
é   as the 'ay' in 'may'
è   as the 'e' in 'merry', but slightly longer
i   as in 'sweet'
o   as in British 'pot'
u   to make this sound, purse you lips as if you were saying 'oo' but make the sound 'ee'

Diphthongs (Vowel Combinations)

ai   as the 'e' in 'bet' but a bit longer
eu   as the 'er' in British 'berth' but shorter
oi   sounds like 'wa'
ui   sounds like 'wi'
au   as the 'o' in 'or'
eau   as the 'ow' in 'show'
ou   as the 'oo' in 'book'

FRENCH

Consonants

These are generally pronounced as they are in English but there are some you should note. Consonants appearing at the end of a word aren't pronounced, unless they run on to a following word.

c   hard, like 'k' before a, o and u
     soft, like 's', before e, i and y
ç   always soft, like 's'
g   hard, as in 'get', before a, o and u
     soft, as in 'germ', before e and i
h   silent
j   as the 's' in measure
q   as 'k'
s   between two vowels, it's pronounced as 'z'
     elsewhere, as the 's' in 'sit'
l   always pronounced with the tip of the tongue touching the back of the upper incisors, and the surface of the tongue higher than for an English 'l'. Be especially careful to maintain this tongue position for 'l's at the ends of words, as in il
r   produced by moving the bulk of the tongue backwards to constrict the air flow in the pharynx, while the tip of the tongue rests behind the lower front teeth. It's quite similar to the noise made by some people before spitting, but with much less friction.

Subject Pronouns

I	je
you	tu (sg & inf)
he/it	il
she/it	elle
we	nous
you	vous (pl & pol)
they	ils/elles (m/f)

FRENCH

Question Words

Why?	Pourquoi?
Which?	Quel?
When?	Quand?
Where?	Où?
Who?	Qui?

MEETING PEOPLE
Greetings & Civilities

Hello./Good morning.	Bonjour.
Goodbye.	Au revoir/Salut.
Good evening.	Bonsoir.
(Have a) good evening.	Bonne soirée.
Good night.	Bonne nuit.
Please.	S'il vous plaît.
Thank you.	Merci.
You're welcome.	De rien/Je vous en prie.
Yes.	Oui.
No.	Non.
No, thank you.	Non, merci.
Excuse me.	Excusez-moi/Pardon.
How are you?	Comment allez-vous/Ça va?
Well, thanks.	Bien, merci.
big/small	grand/petit
open/closed	ouvert/fermé

Making Conversation

What's your name?	Comment vous/appelez-vous?
My name is ...	Je m'appelle ...
How old are you?	Quel âge avez-vous?
I'm 25.	J'ai vingt-cinq ans.

FRENCH

Where are you from?	D'où êtes-vous?
I'm/We're from ...	Je viens/Nous venons ...
America	de l'Amérique
Australia	de l'Australie
Canada	du Canada
England	de l'Angleterre
Germany	de l'Allemagne
Italy	de l'Italie
Japan	du Japon
The Netherlands	des Pays Bas
Spain	de l'Espagne
Sweden	du Suède
Switzerland	de la Suisse

Language Difficulties

Do you speak English?	Parlez-vous anglais?
I understand.	Je comprends.
I don't understand.	Je ne comprends pas.

GETTING AROUND

I want to go to ...	Je veux aller à ...
What is the fare to ...?	Combien coûte le billet pour ...?
How far is ...?	À combien de kilomètres est ...?

FRENCH

When does the ... leave/arrive?	À quelle heure part/arrive ...?
bus	l'autobus
intercity bus/coach	le car
train	le train
boat	le bateau
ferry	le bac

Where's the ...?	Où est ...?
bus station for ...	la gare routière pour ...
train station	la gare
ticket office	la billeterie/le guichet
street	la rue
city	la ville
village	le village
bus stop	l'arrêt d'autobus

Which bus goes to ...?	Quel autobus/car part pour ...?
Does this bus go to ...?	Ce car-là va-t-il à ...?
How many buses per day go to ...?	Il y a combien de cars chaque jour pour ...?
Please tell me when we arrive in ...	Dîtes-moi s'il vous plaît à quelle heure on arrive ...
Stop here, please.	Arrêtez ici, s'il vous plaît.
Please wait for me.	Attendez-moi ici, s'il vous plaît.
May I sit here?	Puis-je m'asseoir ici?
Where can I rent a bicycle?	Où est-ce que je peux louer une bicyclette?

address	adresse
air-conditioning	climatisation
airport	aéroport
camel	chameau
car	voiture
crowded	beaucoup de monde

FRENCH

daily	chaque jour
donkey	âne
horse	cheval
number	numéro
ticket	billet
Wait!	Attendez!

Directions

left/right	gauche/droite
here/there	ici/là
next to	à côté de
opposite	en face
behind	derrière
north	nord
south	sud
east	est
west	ouestici/là

ACCOMMODATION

Where is the hotel?	Où est l'hôtel?
Can I see the room?	Peux-je voir la chambre?
How much is this room per night?	Combien est cette chambre pour une nuit?
Do you have any cheaper rooms?	Avez-vous des chambres moins chères?
That's too expensive.	C'est trop cher.
This is fine.	A va bien.
bed	lit
blanket	couverture
camp site	camping
full	complet
hot water	eau chaude

key	clef/clé
roof	terrasse
room	chambre
sheet	drap
shower	douche
toilet	les toilettes
washbasin	lavabo
youth hostel	auberge de jeunesse

FRENCH

AROUND TOWN

Where is the ...?	Où est ...?
bank	la banque
barber	le coiffeur
beach	la plage
embassy	l'ambassade
market	le marché
mosque	la mosqueé
museum	le museé
old city	le centre historique
palace	le palais
pharmacy	la pharmacie
police station	la police
post office	la poste
restaurant	le restaurant
university	l'université
zoo	le zoo

FRENCH

I want to change ...	Je voudrais changer ...
money	de l'argent
US$	des dollars américains
UK	des livres sterling
A$	des dollars australie
DM	des marks allemands
travellers cheques	des chèques de voyage

INTERESTS

I like ...	J'aime bien ...
caving	la spéléologie
cooking	la cuisine
dancing	la danse
painting	un tableau
singing	le chant
travelling	les voyages

What sort of music do you like?

Quel genre de musique aimes-tu?

What do you think of ...? Qu'est-ce que vous pensez de ...?

I think it's ...	Je pense que c'est ...
boring	ennuyeux
exciting	genial/super
expensive	cher

Drugs

If you find yourself in a situation where drugs are being discussed, the following phrases might help you understand the conversation, but if referring to your own interests, use discretion.

Do you smoke?	Tu fumes?
I'm stoned	Je suis cassé/e.
I'm not interested	Ca ne m'intéresse pas.
I don't take drugs	Je ne prends pas de drogue.

I take ... occasionally	Je prends du (m)/de la (f) ... occasionnellement.
marijuana	à la marijuana
hash	au haschich
heroin	à l'héroïne
cocaine	à la cocaïne
amphetamines	aux amphétamines
acid	à l'acide
drugs	aux drogues

SHOPPING

Where can I buy ...?	Où est-ce que je peux acheter ...?
How much?	Combien?
How much does it cost?	Ça coûte combien?

more/less	plus/moins
too much	trop cher

Do you have (a) ...?	Avez-vous ...?
stamps	des timbres
newspaper	un journal
batteries	des piles
matches	des allumettes
milk	du lait
matches	des allumettes
mineral water	de l'eau minérale

HEALTH

I'm sick.	Je suis malade.
I feel weak.	Je me sens faible.
It hurts here.	J'ai une douleur ici.
I feel nauseous.	J'ai des nausèes.

I have ...	J'ai ...
an allergy	une allergie
diarrhoea	la diarrhèe
influenza	la grippe
a stomachache	mal au ventre
a veneral disease	une maladie venerienne

TIME, DATES & NUMBERS
Time

today	aujourd'hui
tomorrow	demain
yesterday	hier
now	maintenant
morning	matin
afternoon	après-midi
evening	soir
day/night	jour/nuit
week/month/year	semaine/mois/an

What's the time?	Quelle heure est-il?
At what time?	À quelle heure?

after	après
on time	à l'heure
early	tôt
late	tard
quickly	vite
slowly	lentement

FRENCH

Days

Monday	lundi
Tuesday	mardi
Wednesday	mercredi
Thursday	jeudi
Friday	vendredi
Saturday	samedi
Sunday	dimanche

Months

January	janvier
February	février
March	mars
April	avril
May	mai
June	juin
July	juillet
August	août
September	septembre
October	octobre
November	novembre
December	décembre

Cardinal Numbers

0	zéro	10	dix
1	un	11	onze
2	deux	12	douze
3	trois	13	treize
4	quatre	14	quatorze
5	cinq	15	quinze
6	six	16	seize
7	sept	17	dix-sept
8	huit	18	dix-huit
9	neuf	19	dix-neuf

FRENCH

20	vingt	100	cent
21	vingt-et-un	101	cent un
22	vingt-deux	125	cent vingt-cinq
30	trente	200	deux cents
40	quarante	300	trois cents
50	cinquante	400	quatre cents
60	soixante	1000	mille
70	soixante-dix	2000	deux milles
80	quatre-vingts	3000	trois milles
90	quatre-vingt-dix	4000	quatre milles

Ordinal Numbers

first	premier	eighth	huitième
second	deuxième	ninth	neufième
third	troisième	tenth	dixième
fourth	quatrième	twentieth	vingtième
fifth	cinquième	thirtieth	trentième
sixth	sixième	fortieth	quarantième
seventh	septième	fiftieth	cinquantième

EMERGENCIES

Call a doctor!	Appelez un médecin!
Call the police!	Appelez la police!
Help me please!	Au secours/Aidez-moi!
Thief!	(Au) voleur!

EMERGENCIES

Help!	ʿteqnī!	!عتقني
Stop!	wqef!	!وقف
Go away!	sīr fhalek!	!سير فحالك
Thief!	sheffar!	!شفار
Fire!	lʿafiya!	!العافية
Danger	khâtâr	خطر
Help me please!	ʿawennī ʿafak!	!عاوني عفاك
Emergency!	'mestaʿzhel!	!مستعجل
Where's the toilet?	fīn kein lbīt lma?	فين كان البيت الماء؟
I'm lost	tweḍḍert	توضرت

Can I use the telephone?
wakha nstaʿmel ttīlifūn?
واش نستعمل التليفون؟

I've lost my ...	tweḍḍer līya (m) ...	... توضر لي
	tweḍḍeraṭ līya (f) ...	... توضرت لي
	tweḍḍerū līya (pl) ...	... توضرو لي
daughter	bentī	بنتي
son	weldī	ولدي
bags	lhwayezh	الحوايج
handbag	ssak	ساك
money	lflūs	الفلوس
passport	lpaspūr	الباسبور
travellers cheques	shikat seyahīya	شيكات سياحية
wallet	bezṭām	بزطام

There's been an accident!

ūqʿat ksīda!

وقعت كسيدة!

Call a doctor!

ʿayyeṭ ʿla shī ṭbīb!

عيط علي شي طبيب!

Call an ambulance!

ʿayyeṭ ʿla ssayyara del'asʿaf!

عيط علي السيارة دال اسعاف!

I have medical insurance.

ʿandī lasūrans dyal ṣṣhha

عندي لاسورانس ديال الصحة

I'm ill.

ana mreiḍ (m)

انا مريض

ana mreiḍa (f)

انا مريضة

Contact (next of kin).

ttaṣel b (shī wahed men lʿā'īla)

تصل ب شي واحد من العاءلة

I'll call the police!

ghādī nʿeyyaṭ ʿla lbūlīs!

غادي نعيط علي البوليس!

Call the police!

ʿayyeṭ ʿla lbūlīs!

عيط علي البوليس!

Where's the police station?

fīn keina lkumesarīya?

فين كاينة الكوميساريا؟

Someone robbed me!

serqna shī wahed!

سرقني شي واحد!

DEALING WITH THE POLICE

My ... was stolen.	tesreq līya ... dyalī	تسرق لي ... ديالي
bags	shshwaksh	شواكش
handbag	ssak	ساك
money	lflūs	الفلوس
papers/documents	lweraq	وراق
passport	lpaspōr	لباسبور
travellers cheques	shekat ssīyahī	الشيكات السياحية
wallet	lbezṭām	لبزطام

I've been assaulted/raped.

thzhem ʿlīya/ghtaṣabunī   تهجم علي / غتصبوني

I've been robbed.

tsreqt   تسرقت

I didn't do anything.

madert walū   مادرت والو

We're innocent.

hna 'abrīya'a   حنا ابرياء

I want to call my embassy/consulate.

bghīt nʿeyyet l ssīfara/   بغيت نعيط علي السفارة /
lkunsūlīya   القنصلية

Can I call someone?

wash yemkenlī nʿeyyet tiltifūn?   واش يمكن لي نعيط علي واحد؟

I want a lawyer who speaks English.

bghīt wahed lmuhamī llī   بغيت واحد المحامي الي
keitkellem neglīzīya   كيتكلم انكليزية

EMERGENCIES

GROWL!

When comes before a vowel, the vowel is 'growled' from the back of the throat. If it's before a consonant or at the end of a word, it sounds like a glottal stop.

EMERGENCIES

I understand.		
fhemt		فهمت
I don't understand.		
mafhemtsh		مافهمتش
I'm sorry, forgive me.		
smeh līya		سمح لي
I've been arrested.		
thebst		تحبست
What am I accused of?		
bash mthūm?		باش متهم؟

cell	lbenniqa	لبنيقة
jail	hebs	الجبس
judge	qadī	قاضي
guilty	mthūm	متهم
not guilty	barī	باريء
lawyer	muhamī	محامي
police officer	bulīsī	بوليسي
police station	kumīsarīya	كميسارية
prison	hebs	حبس
murder	qtīla	قتيلا
rape	ighteṣāb	اغتصاب
stealing	serqa	سرقة
traffic violation	khṭīya	خطية
trial	hukem	حكم
working without authorisation	khadem bla lwuraq	خادم بلا الوراق

ENGLISH – MOROCCAN ARABIC

A

English	Moroccan Arabic	Arabic
able (can)	qder	قدر
above	fuq	فوق
abroad	kharezh	الخارج
to accept	qbel	قبل
accident	ksida	كسيدة
accommodation	'iqama	إقامة
across	qbalt	قبلت
address	'unwun'	عنوان
to admire	qedder	قدر
admission	'i'tiraf	اعتراف
to admit	'tarf	اعرف
adult	balgh	البالغ
advantage	mzīya	مزية
advice	nāṣiha	نصيحة
aeroplane	ṭeiyāra	طيارة
after	men b'd	من بعد
after-shave	rīha	ريحة
afternoon	'shīya	عشية
again	'awed tanī	عاودتاني
against	ḍed	ضد
age	'mer	عمر
aggressive	w'er	واعر
to agree	ttafq	اتفق
Agreed! mtafqīn!		متفقين
agriculture	filaha	فلاحة
ahead	qeddam	قدام
aid (help)	'awen	عون
AIDS	sīda	سيدا
air	hwa	هواء
air-conditioning	klīmatī-zasīyun	كليماتيزسيون
air mail	betṭeiyāra	بالطيارة
airport	maṭār	مطار
airport tax	darība dyal maṭār	ضريبة ديال المطار
alarm clock	feyyaq	الفياق
all	kūlshī	كول شي
allergy	hasasīya	حساسية
to allow	smeh	سمح
almost	tqrīban	تقريبا
alone	būwhedī	بوحدي
already	b'da	بعد
also	htta	حتى
altitude	'ulu	العلو
always	dīma	ديما
amateur	hawī	هاوي
ambassador	safir	سفير
America	amrīka	امريكا
among	bīn	بين
ancient	qdīm	قديم
and	ū-	او
angry	gheḍban	غضبان
animal	hayawan	حيوان
annual	'am l 'am	عام ل عام
another one	wahed akhūr	واحد اخور
answer (n)	zhawab	جواب
ant	nemla	نملة
antibiotics	'antībīyutik	انتيبيوتيك
antique	'areq	عريق
any	shī	شي
apple	teffah	تفاح
appointment	mī'ad	ميعاد
approximately	tqrīban	تقريبا
archaeology	'lim dyal latar	علم ديال الاثار
architect	muhendīs	مهندس
architecture	handasa	هندسة
to argue	tkhaṣem	تخاصم
arm	dra'	دراع
around	zhwayeh	جوايح
arrival	wṣul	وصول
to arrive	wṣel	وصل
art	fenn	فن
artist	fennan	فنان
ashtray	tfaya	طفاية
to ask	sewwel	سول
asleep	na'es	ناعس
aspirin	asprīn	اسبيرين
atmosphere	zhew	الجو
aunt (paternal)	'emma	عمة
(maternal)	khala	خالة
Australia	astrāliya	استراليا
autumn (fall)	khrīf	خريف

English	Transliteration	Arabic
avenue	sharîᶜ	شاريع
awake	fayeq	فايق
awful	khayb	خايب

B

English	Transliteration	Arabic
baby	derri şghîr	دري صغير
baby food	makla dyal drari sghar	مكلة ديال ردراري صغار
babysitter	murabbiya dyal drari sghar	ربية ديال م درادي صغار
back	lör	لور
back (body)	ḍher	ضهر
backpack	sakaḍō	ساكاضو
bad	khaib	خايب
bag	khensha	خنشة
bag	sak	ساك
baggage	bagazh	باكاج
bakery	ferran	فران
balcony	balkön	بلكون
ball	kura	كرة
ballet	qurtasa	قرطسة
banana	banan	بنان
band (music)	mezhmuᶜ	مجموعة
bandage	faşma	فاصمة
bank	bānka	بنك
barber	hellaq	حلاق
basket	sella	سلة
bath	hemmam	حمام
bathing suit	mayyu	مايو
bathroom	bît lma	بيت الماء
bathtub	hemmam	حمام
battery	batrî	بتري
beach	laplazh	لابلاج
beans (green)	lūbīya	لوبية
beautiful	zwîn	زوين
because	ᶜla qîbal	علي قبال
bed	namūsîya	نموسية
bedroom	bît nnᶜas	بيت نعاس
bee	nehla	نحلة
beef	begrî	بكري
beer	bîra	بيرا

before	qbel	قبل
beggar	ṭallab	طلاب
to begin	bda	بدا
behind	mura	مورا
below	teht	تحت
beside	zhenb	جنب
best	rfeᶜ	رفيع
to bet	tkhater	تخاتر
better	hessen	حسن
between	ma bîn	مابين
bicycle	beshklîṭā	بشكليطة
big	kbîr	كبير
bill	faktūra	فكتورة
binoculars	shūwafat	شوفات
bird	ṭeir	طير
birth certificate	ᶜaqed lizdiyad	عقد لزدياد
birthday	ᶜîd lmîlad	عيد الميلاد
biscuits	helwat	حلوة
bite	ᶜeḍḍa	عضة
to bite	ᶜeḍḍ	عض
black	khel	كحل
blanket	bṭṭānîya	بطانية
to bleed	seyyel ddemm	سيل الدم
to bless	rHem	رحم
blind	ᶜma	عمي
blood	demm	الدم
blood group	nnuᶜ dyal ddemm	نوع ديال الدم
blood test	duwwez ddemm	دوز الدم
blue	zerq	زرق
boat	flūka	فلوكة
body	zhesm	جسم
to boil	sleq	سلق
boiled	mslūq	مسلوق
Bon appétit!	besha ū rraha	بصحة و راحة
Bon voyage!	ṭrîq ssalama	طريق السلامة
bone	ᶜḍem	عضم
book	ktab	كتاب
bookshop	mektaba	مكتبة

C

boots	butiyun	بوتيو
border	hdada	حدود
bored	meqnuṭ	مقنوط
boring	mqnaṭ	مقناط
to borrow	tsellef	تسلف
both	bzhūzh	ب جوج
bottle	qerᶜa	قرعة
bottle opener	lfttaha	الفتاحة
boulevard	shariᶜ	شاريع
bowl	zlafa	زلفة
box	senduq	صندوق
box (cardboard)	kartūna	كرطونة
boxing	lbōks	بوكس
boy	weld	ولد
boyfriend	saheb	صاحب
bracelet	deblizh	دبليج
brass	nhas ṣfer	نحاس اصفر
brave	shzhiᶜ	شجيع
bread	khūbz	خبز
to break	herres	هرس
breakable	iqder itherres	اقدر اتهرس
breakfast	fṭur	فطور
to breathe	nfes	نفس
bribe	reshwa	رشوة
bridge	qenṭra	قنطرة
to bring	zhīb	جيب
broken	mherres	مهرس
broom	sheṭṭāba	شطابة
brother	akh	اخ
brown	qehwī	قهوي
to bruise	tqesseh	تقصح
brush	shīta	شيتا
bucket	sṭel	سطل
Buddhist	būḍī	بودي
bug	hashara	حشرة
to build	bnī	بني
building	bnī	البني
burn	herqa	حريق
bus (city)	ṭōbīs	طوبيس
bus (intercity)	kar	كار
bus station	meheṭṭa	محطة
bus stop	blaṣa dyal	بلكة ديال
	ṭṭōbīsat	الطوبيسات

business	tizhara	تجارة
businessperson	tazher	تاجر
busy	meshghūl	مشغول
but	walakīn	ولكن
butter	zebda	زبدة
butterfly	fertattu	فرتاتو
buttermilk	lben	لبن
buttons	ṣḍāf	صضاف
to buy	shrī	شري

C

cabbage	krum	كروم
calendar	yawmīya	يومية
calm	hani	هاني
camel	zhmel	جمل
camera	ṣṣuwwara	صورة
camera shop	ssuwwar	صوار
to camp	khiyyem	خيم
campsite	mukhayyam	مخيم
can (aluminium)	huk	حوك
can (be able)	qder	قدر
can opener	hellala	حلالة
Canada	kanada	كند
to cancel	lgha	لغ
candle	shmaᶜa	شمعة
car	ṭumubīl	طموبيل
cards	karta	كرط
care (about)	htam	هتم
Careful!		
redd balek!		رد بالك
carpet	zerbīya	زربية
to carry	hez	هز
carton	karṭōn	كرطون
cashier	mzher dyal	مجر
	flūs	ديال الفلوس
cassette	kassiṭ	كسيت
castle	qṣer	قصر
cat	meshsh	مش
cave	ghar	غار
to celebrate	htafel	احتفل
centimetre	ṣāntīm	سنتيم
ceramic	zhellizh	جليج
certificate	shhada	شهادة

chair	kūrsī	كرسي
chance	furṣa	فرصة
to change	ṣerref	صرّف
change (coins)	ṣerf	صرف
cheap	rkheiṣ	رخيص
to cheat	gheshsh	غش
to check	qelleb	قلب
check-in (desk)	mektab dyal tszhīl	مكتب ديال التسجيل
cheese	frumazh	فرماج
chemist	lfārmasyan	الفرماسيان
chess	strunzh	سترنج
chest	sder	صدر
chewing gum	mska	مسكة
chicken	dzhazh	دجاج
child	derrī ؛	دري
children	drerri	دراري
chocolate	sheklāṭ	شكلاط
to choose	khtar	ختار
Christian	masīhī	مسيحي
church	kanīsa	كنيسة
cigarettes	garru	كارو
cinema	sīnīma	سينما
circus	sīrk	سيرك
citizenship	zhensīya	جنسية
city	mdīna	مدينة
city centre	wuṣṭ lmdīna	وسط المدينة
civil rights	qanūn lmadanī	قانون المدني
class	qsem	قسم
clean	nqī	نقي
to clean	neddef	نضف
clear (understood)	ṣāfī	صافي
client	klīyan	كليان
cliff	skher	صخر
to climb	tleˁ	اطلع
clock	magana	ماكانة
to close	sedd	سد
closed	mesdūd	مسدود
clothing	hawayzh	حوايج
clothing store	mahal dyal lhawayzh	محل ديال الحوايج

cloud	ḍbaba	ضباب
coast	muhīṭ	محيط
coat	kbōṭ	كبوط
coffee	qehwa	قهوة
coins	ṣerf	صرف
coke	kōka	كوكا
cold (adj)	bared	بارد
cold (illness)	mrewweh	مروح
cold water	lma bared	الماء بارد
colleague	zmīl	زميل
college	zhamīˁ	جامعة
colour	lūn	لون
comb	meshṭa	مشطة
come!	azhi!	اجي!
come	zha	جا
comedy	frazha	فرجة
comfortable	mreyyeh	مريح
comics	nukat	نكات
commerce	tīzhara	تجارة
companion	sahb	صاحب
company	sharīka	شركة
compass	bōṣala	بوصلة
complaint	shekwa	شكوة
computer	muhasīb	محاسب
concert	shra	سهرة
confirm (booking)	hzhez	حجز
congratulations	mbrūk	مبروك
conservative	muhafid	محافظ
constipation	tˁsam	تعصام
construction work	bnī	البني
consulate	quṣūlīya	قنصلية
contact lenses	ˁadasat dyal shshūf	عدسات ديال الشوف
contraceptives	dwa ded lhmel	دوي ضد الحمل
contract	kuntra	كونطرا
cook	tbakh	طباخ
to cook	ṭeyyeb	طيب
copper	nhas hmer	نحاس احمر
corner	qent	قنت
corrupt	reshwī	رشاوي

D

English	Transliteration	Arabic
cost	taman	ثمن
to cost	swa	سوي
cotton	qten	قطن
cough	keha	كحة
to count	hseb	حسب
country	blad	بلاد
country market	sūq	سوق
countryside	badīya	بادية
coupon	bun	البون
court (legal)	mhkama	محكمة
(tennis)	tīran dyal tinīs	تران ديال تنيس
cow	begra	بكرة
crafty	hraymī	حرايمي
crazy	hemq	حمق
credit card	kart krīdī	كارت كريدي
cross-country trail	rīf	ريف
cross (angry)	kʿa	كعا
crossroad	kerwazma	كروزمة
crowded	zham	زحام
cup	kas	كاس
curtain	khamīya	خامية
customs	ʿadat	عادات
customs official	dīwānī	ديواني
to cut	qṭʿ	قطع

D

English	Transliteration	Arabic
dad	bba	با
daily	yawmīyyan	يوميا
damp	fazeg	فازك
to dance	shṭeh	شطح
dancing	shṭīh	شطيح
dangerous	khāṭār	خطر
dark	ḍlem	ضلم
dark (colour)	meghlūq	مغلوق
date	tarīkh	تاريخ
date of birth	nhar zzīyada	نهار زيادة
daughter	bent	بنت
dawn	fzher	فجر
day	nhar	نهار

day after tomorrow beʿd ghedda		غدا بعد
day before yesterday wel lbareh		اول بارح
dead	miyyet	ميت
deaf	smek	سمك
to deal	tʿamel	تعامل
death	mūt	موت
to decide	qerrer	قرر
deep	ghareq	غارق
deer	kurkdan	كركدان
to delay	ʿtel	عطل
delicious	bnin	بنين
delirious	thaṭīr	تهاطير
democracy	dimūqāṭīya	دموقراطية
dentist	ṭbīb dyal ssnan	طبيب ديال السنان
to deny	refḍ	رفض
deodorant	rīha	ريحة
to depart	khrezh	خرج
departure	dahab	دهاب
descendent	men ssulala	من سلالة
desert	ṣehra	سحراء
destination	tizhan	اتجاه
to destroy	heddem	هدم
detail	tefṣīl	تفاصيل
diabetic	fīh sukkar	فيه سكر
diaper	khruq	خروق
diarrhoea	kersh zharīya	جارية كرش
diary	mudakkīra	مذكرة
dictionary	munzhid	منجد
to die	mat	مات
different	mekhtalef	مختلف
difficult	ṣʿeib	صعب
dinner	ʿsha	عشاء
direct	nīshan	نيشان
director	mudīr	مدير
dirt	trāb	طراب
dirty	mwessekh	موسخ
disabled	muʿewweq	معوق
discount	tekhfīd	تخفيض

E

to discover	ktashef	كتشف
discrimination	'unṣuriya	عنصرية
disease	merḍa	مرضة
dismissal	merfōḍ	مرفوض
dizzy	dūkha	دوخة
to do	dar	دار
doctor	ṭbīb	طبيب
documentary	wata'iq	وثايق
dog	kelb	كلب
doll	munīka	منيكة
donkey	hmar	حمار
door	bab	باب
double	zhuzh	جوج
double bed	srīr dyal zhuzh	سرير ديال جوج
double room	bīt dyal zhuzh	بيت ديال جوج
dozen	zīna	زنة
drama	ma'sat	ماسات
to dream	hlem	حلم
dress	keswa	كسوة
to dress	lbes	لبس
to drink	shreb	شرب
to drive	ṣāg	ساق
driver's licence	permī	برمي
to drop	ṭeyyeh	طيح
drugs	mukhdīrat	مخدرات
drum	ṭbel	طبل
drunk (adj)	sekran	سكران
dry (adj)	nashef	ناشف
to dry	nshef	نشف
dull	hafi	حافي
dummy (pacifier)	skata	سكاتة
dust	ghubra	غبرة
duty	wazheb	واجب

E

English	Transliteration	Arabic
each (one)	kūl wahed	كل واحد
ear	wden	ودن
early	bekrī	بكري
to earn	rbeh	ربح
earrings	twaneg	طوانك
ears	wednīn	ودنين
earth	denya	دنيا
earth (soil)	lerḍ	لرض
earthquake	zelzla	زلزال
east	sherq	شرق
easy	sahel	سهل
to eat	kla	كلي
Eat!	kūl!	كول!
economic	qtiṣādī	اقتصادي
economy	qtiṣad	اقتصاد
editor	nashir	ناشر
educated	qarī	قاري
education	te'līm	تعلم
eggs	beiḍ	بيض
election	intikhab	انتخاب
electricity	ḍu	ضو
elevator	sansūr	سنسور
embarrassed	hshem	حشم
embarrassment	hshūma	حشومة
embassy	sīfāra	السفارة
embroidery	terz	طرز
emergency	musta'zhel	مستعجل
employee	kheddam	خدام
employer	baṭrōn	بترون
empty	khawī	خاوي
end	akher	اخر
engagement	muwafaqat zzawazh	موافقة الزواج
engine	muṭōr	مطور
engineer	mūhendis	مهندس
engineering	handasa	هندسة
England	anglatīra	انكلترا
English	neglīzīya	انكلنزي
enjoy (oneself)	nsheṭ 'la rasek	نشط علي راسك
enough	kafi	كافي
enter	dkhel	دخل
entertaining	tenshīṭ	تنشط
entrance	dekhla	دخلة
envelope	zhwa	جوي
environment	bī'a	بيئة
epilepsy	larīh	لرياح
equal	bhal bhal	بحال بحال

156

F

equipment	tezhīz	تجهيز
essential	ḍarurī	ضروري
Europe	ūruba	اوروبا
European	ūrubī	اوروبي
even so		
wekhkha dak shī		وخ داكشي
evening	ʿshīya	عشية
every day	kūl nhar	كل نهار
everything	kūl shī	كولشي
exact	huwa hadak	هو هدك
example	mītal	متل
excellent	rfīʿ	رفيع
exchange	tebdīl	تبديل
exchange rate		
qīma dyal ṣṣerf		قيمة ديال الصرف
excluded	mṭruḍ	مطرود
excuse (n)	ʿder	عدر
Excuse me.		
smeh līya		سمح لي
to exhibit	ʿerḍ	عرض
exhibition	ʿarḍ	عرض
exit	khurouzh	الخروج
expensive	ghalī	غالي
experience	tezhrība	تجربة
exploitation	ʿistighlal	استغلال
express	sarīʿ	سريع
express mail		
lbared lʿazhīl		البريد العاجل
extra	zayed	زايد
eye	ʿeyn	عين

F

fabric	tūb	توب
face	wzheh	وجه
factory	mʿmel	معمل
to faint	skhef	سخف
fair	mnaseb	مناسب
fake	mzwwer	مزور
fall (autumn)	khrīf	الخريف
family	ʿaʾīla	عائلة

famous	mshhōr	مشهور
fan	reyyaha	رياحة
fans (of team)	muhib	محب
far	bʿeid	بعيد
farm	firma	فرمة
farmer	fellah	فلاح
fast (adj)	dghīya	دغي
to fast	ṣām	صام
fat	ghled	غليض
father	walid	والد
father-in-law	nsīb	نسيب
faucet (tap)	rōbīnī	روبيني
fault (someone's)	ghalaṭ	غلط
fear	khūf	خوف
to feel	hess	حس
feelings	ʿihsas	احساس
fence	mukhliweḍ	مخلوض
festival	musem	موسم
fever	skhana	سخانة
few	qlīl	قليل
fiancée/fiancé	khaṭīb/	خطيب /
	khatiba	خطيبة
fiction	khayalī	خيالي
field (land)	ʿerḍ	الأرض
to fight	ḍḍarb	ضارب
to fill	ʿammer	عمر
film	fīlm	فيلم
filtered	mṣeffī	مصفي
to find	lga	لكا
fine	zwīn	زوين
finger	ṣbeʿ dyal	صبع
	yeddʿ	ديال اليد
Finish!		
kemmel!		كمل !
fire	ʿafīya	عافية
firewood	hṭeb	حطب
first	luwwel	للول
fish	hōt	حوت
fish shop	hanūt dyal	لحانوت
	lhōṭ	اديال الحوت
flag	raya	راية
flashlight	pīl	بيل
flat (land, etc)	waṭiya	واطية

flea	beq	بق
flight	ṭeiyara	طيارة
floor	'erḍ	الأرض
floor (storey)	ṭebqa	طبقة
flour	dgīg	دكيك
flower	werḍa	وردة
flower seller	mūl lwerḍ	مول الورد
to fly	ṭār	طار
fly (insect)	debbana	دبانة
follow	tbeʿ	تبع
food	makla	مكلة
foot	rzhel	رجل
football (soccer)	kōra	الكرة
footpath	mrīra	مريرة
foreign	azhnabī	اجنبي
foreigner	azhnabī	اجنبي
forest	ghaba	غابة
forever	dīma	ديما
to forget	nsa	نسي
to forgive	smeḥ	سمح
fork	fershetta	فرشطة
fortnight	kanza	الكانزة
fortune teller	shuwwaf	شواف
fountain	khʿṣṣa	خصة
fourth	rūbūʿ	ربع
free (not busy)	msalī	مسالي
free (of charge)	fābōr	فابور
freedom	ḥurrīya	حرية
to freeze	tellezh	تلج
fresh	ṭrei	طري
Friday	zhzhemʿa	الجمعة
fried	meqlī	مقلي
friend	ṣāḥeb	صاحب
front	qeddam	قدام

| frozen foods | | |
| makla mtelzha | | مكلة متلجة |

fruit	fakīya	فاكية
full	ʿamer	عامر
fun	nashāṭ	نشاط
funeral	gnaza	كنازة
future	mūstèqbal	مستقبل

G

game	leʿba	لعبة
garage	garazh	كراج
garbage	zbel	ذبل
garden	zharda	جردة
gardening	teswab dyal	تصواب
	zherda	ديال الجردة
garlic	tūma	تومة
gas cartridge	bōṭa dyal	بوطة
	lgaz	ديال الكاز
gate	bab	باب
general	ʿamm	عام
germ	mīkrūb	مكروب
German	almanī	الماني
Germany	almanīya	المانية

| Get lost! | | |
| sīr fehalek! | | سير ف حالك! |

gift	hdīya	هدية
girl	bent	بنت
girlfriend	ṣaḥba	صاحبة
to give	ʿṭa	عط
glass	zhazh	جاج
glass (drinking)	kas	كاس
glasses (eye)	nḍāder	ندادر
glue	lṣāq	لساق
to go	msha	مشي
go away	sīr fhalek	سر فحالك

| Go straight ahead. | | |
| sīr nīshan | | سر نيشان |

goal	hadaf	هدف
goat	meʿza	معزة
God	llah	الله
gold	dheb	دهب
good	mezyan	مزيان
goodbye	bessalama	سلامة
government	ḥūkūma	حكومة
gram	gram	كرام
grandchild	ḥafīd	حفيد
grandfather	zhedd	الجد
grandmother	zhedda	الجدة

grape	ʿneb	عنب
grass	rbiʿ	ربيع
grave	qbur	قبر
Great!		
bikhīr!		بخير!
green	khḍer	خضر
greengrocer	mul lkhuḍra	مول الخضرة
grey	rmadi	رمادي
guardian	ʿssas	عساس
to guess	qedder	قدر
guest	ḍeif	ضيف
guide (n)	gīd	كيد
guitar	gītar	كيطار
gum	mska	مسكة
gym	qaʿa dyal	قاعة
	rīyaḍa	ديال الرياضة
gymnastics	rīyaḍa	رياضة

H

habit	ʿada	عادة
hair	shʿr	شعر
hairbrush	meshta dyal	مشطة
	shshʿar	ديال الشعر
half	neṣṣ	نص
hammer	mṭerqa	مطرقة
hand	yedd	يد
handbag	sak	صاك
handicrafts	harayfīya	حريفية
handmade	belyedd	باليد
handsome	zwīn	زوين
happy	ferhan	فرحان
harbour	merṣa	مرسى
hard	qaṣeh	قاصح
harass	shṭen	شطن
hat	terbūsh	طربوش
have	ʿand	عند
he	huwwa	هو
head	rāṣ	الراس
headache	hrīq raṣ	حريق راس
health	ṣehha	صحة
hear	smeʿ	سمع
hearing aid	semmaʿa	سماعة

heart	qelb	قلب
heat	ṣehd	صهد
heater	sekhkhana	سخانة
heavy	tqil	تقيل
Hello! (answering telephone)		
alō		آلو
Hello.		
labas		لاباس
helmet	kask	كاسك
help	mūsaʿada	مساعدة
to help	ʿawen	عاون
Help me!		
ʿawenni!		عاوني!
herbalist	ʿashshab	عشاب
herbs	ʿazhūb	العشوب
here	hna	هنا
high	ʿali	عالي
high school	tanawī	الثانوي
hill	tal	تل
Hindu	hendī	هندي
hire (rent)	kra	كراء
historical ruins	ʾatar	الآتار
hitchhike	lutuṣtub	لطسطب
hole	teqbu	تقبة
holiday	ʿuṭla	عطلة
homeless	msherred	المشرد
honest	mʿqūl	معقول
honey	ʿsel	عسل
horrible	khayeb	خايب
horse	ʿawd	العود
horse riding	rkub lkhīl	ركوب الخيل
hospital	ṣbiṭār	سبيطار
hot	skhūn	سخون
hot (spicy)	harr	حار
hot water	lma skhūn	لما سخون
hotel	ūṭeil	لوتيل
hour	saʿa	ساعة
house	dar	دار
housework	khedma	خدمة ديال
	dyal ddar	الدار
How?		
kīfash?		كفاش؟

hug	ʿenneq	عنق
human rights	ḥuqq l-insan	حق الانسان
hundred	mya	مية
hungry	zhīʿan	جعان
Hurry up! serbi!		سربي!
husband	razhel	رجل

I

ice	telzh	تلج
ice cream	laglas	لكلاس
idea	fikra	فكرة
identification	teʿrīf	تعريف
identification card	biṭaqa ttaʿrīf	بطاقة تعريف
if	ila	إلا
ill	mrīḍḍ	مريض
immediately	fissaʿ	فساع
immigration	hizhra	هجرة
important	muhimm	مهم
industry	sinaʿa	صناعة
information	meʿlūmat	معلومات
inject	hqen	حقن
injection	shūka	شوكة
injury	zherha	جرحة
inside	dakhel	لداخل
inspector	mūfettish	مفتش
instructor	murshīd	مرشد
insurance	lāṣurānṣ	لصورنس
intense	shdīd	شديد
interesting	mūhī	مهم
intermission	istiraha	استراحة
international	ʿalamī	عالمي
interview	istezhwab	استجواب
island	zhazīra	جزيرة
itch (n)	hkka	حكة
itinerary	ṭrīq	طريق

J

jacket	kebbuṭ	كبوت
jail	hebs	حبس
jam	kufîtir	كوفيتير
jar	gherraf	غراف
jealous	hessad	حساد
jeans	dzhzhin	دجين
jewellery	bīzhū	بيجو
Jewish	ihudī	ايهودي
job (work)	khedma	خدمة
joke	nekta	نكتة
to joke	ḍhek	ضحك
journalist	ṣāhāfī	صحافي
journey	safar	سفر
judge	qaḍī	قاضي
juice	ʿaṣeir	عصير
to jump	nqez	نقز
Just a minute. wahed dqīqa		واحد دقيقة
justice	ʿedala	عدالة

K

key	sarūt	ساروت
keyboard	ʿaddad	العداد
to kick	rkel	ركل
to kill	qtel	قتل
kilogram	kīlū	كيلو
kilometre	kīlūmīter	كيلومتر
kind	ḍrīf	طريف
king	malik	ملك
kiss	būsa	بوسة
to kiss	bas	باس
kitchen	kūzina	كوزينة
kitten	mshisha	مشيشة
knapsack	şakaḍō	صاك آضو
knee	rekba	ركبة
knife	mūs	موس
to knock	deqq	دق
to know	ʿref	عرف

L

lace	sīr	سير
lake	ḍaya	ضاية
lamb	ghenmī	غنمي
land	ʿerḍ	ارض

language	lūgha	لغة
large	kbīr	كبير
last (final)	akhīr	اخير
late	mᶜettel	معطل
to laugh	dhek	ضحك
launderette	mesbana	مصبنة
law	qanūn	قانون
lawyer	mūhamī	محامي
lay down		
tekka		تقة
lazy	fenyan	فنيان
leader	raᶜis	ريس
learn	tᶜellem	تعلم
leather	zheld	جلد
left (not right)	līser	ليسر
leg	rzhel	رجل
legalisation	muwafaq	موفق
lemon	hamed	حامض
length	tul	طول
lens	zhzha	الجاجة
less	qell	قل
Let's go.		
yallah		يالاه
letter	bra	برا
liar	keddab	كذاب
library	khīzana	خزانة
lice	gmel	كمل
to lie	kdeb	كذب
life	hayat	حياة
lift (elevator)	sensūr	سنسور
light (sun/lamp)	du	ضو
(weight)	khfif	خفيف
(colour)	meftūh	مفتوح
light bulb	bula	بولة
like (similar)	bhal	بحال
to like	bgha	بغي
line	sherta	شرطة
lips	shlaqem	شلاقم
lipstick	ᶜker	لعكر
listen	smeᶜ	سمع
little (amount)	qlīl	قليل
(small)	shwīya	شوي

little bit		
shī shwīya		شي شوي
live (somewhere) saken		ساكن
local	mahalī	محلي
location	mawqiᶜ	موقع
lock	qfel	قفل
to lock	sedd	سد
long	twīl	طويل
to look	shaf	شاف
Look!		
shūf!		شوف!
loose	metlūq	مطلوق
loose change	sserf	صرف
lose	twedder	توضر
loser	khaser	خاسر
loss	khesran	خسران
lost	talf	تالف
loud	mzhehhed	مجهد
love	hebb	حب
lover	hbīb	حبيب
low	habt	هابط
loyal	sadiq	صادق
luck	zher	زهر
luggage	hwayezh	حوايج
lump	kutla	كتلة
lunch	ghda	غدا
lunchtime	weqt lgheda	وقت الغدا
luxury	rafahīya	رفاهية

M

machine	makīna	ماكينة
mad	msetti	مصطي
made (of)	mesnūᶜ	مصنوع من
	men	
magazine	mazhella	مجلة
magician	sehhar	سحار
mail	bared	بريد
mailbox	sendūq dyal	صندوق
	lbrawat	ديال البروات
mailman	faktur	فكتور
majority	aghlabīya	اغلبية

make-up	tezhmīl	تجميل
make	ṣaweb	صوب
make fun of		
dhek 'la		ضحك علي
male	dker	دكر
man	razel	راجل
manager	musayyer	مسير
many	bezzaf	بزاف
map	kharīta	خريطة
market	sūq	سوق
marriage	zwazh	زواج
married	mzewwezh	مزوج
to marry	zuwwezh	زوج
marvellous	ʿazhīb	عجيب
mat	hṣira	حصيرة
matches	wqeid	وقيد
mattress	mḍerreba	مضربة
maybe	yemken	يمكن
meaning	meʿna	معنى
meat	lhem	لحم
mechanic	mikanīsiyan	ميكانيسيان
medal	midaya	مداية
medicine	dwa	دواء
to meet	tlaqa mʿa	تلق مع
member	ʿuḍō	عضو
menstruation	weqt ddemm	وقت الدم
menu	wezhba	وجبة
message	mīṣāzh	مساج
metal	ṣulb	صلب
metre	mītrū	ميترو
midnight	tnash dllīl	تناش دليل
migraine	shqīqa	شقيقة
military	ʿaskarīya	عسكرية
milk	hlīb	حليب
millimetre	milmeter	ملمتر
million	melyūn	مليون
mind	ʿqel	عقل
mineral water	lma maʿdīnī	ماء معدنية
mint tea	'atī	اتاي
	bennaʿnaʿ	بنعنع
minute	dqīqa	دقيقة
mirror	mraya	مراية

miss (feel absence)	twehhesh	توحش
mistake	ghalṭa	غلطة
to mix	khelleṭ	خلط
moisturising cream	dhna dyal luwzhih	دهنة ديال الوجه
money	flūs	فلوس
monkey	qerd	قرد
month	shher	شهر
monument	atar	آثار
moped	muṭur	موتور
moon	gmra	قمر
more	kter	كتر
morning	ṣbah	صباح
mosque	zhameʿ	جامع
mother	walīda	والدة
mother-in-law	nsība	نسيبة
motorcycle	muṭur	موتور
mountain	zhbel	جبل
mountain range	silsila dyal zhzhbal	سلسلة ديال جبال
mouse	far	فار
mouth	fūmm	فم
movie	film	فلم
mud	ghīs	غيس
mule	bghel	بغل
Mum	mmī	مي
muscle	ʿadala	عضلة
museum	methef	متحف
music	mūsīqa	موسيقى
musician	musīqar	موسيقار
Muslim	meslem	مسلم
mute	zanzōn	زنزون
mutton	ghenm	غنمي

N

name	smīya	سمي
nappy	khruq	خروق
nationality	zhensīya	جنسية
nature	ṭabīyʿa	طبيعة
near	qrīb	قريب
necessary	lazem	لازم

English	Moroccan Arabic	Arabic
necklace	sensla	سنسلة
to need (sewing)	htazh	حتاج
needle (sewing)	ïbra	ابرا
(syringe)	ïbra	ابرا
neighbour	zhar	جار
neither	hetta wahed	حتى واحد
net	shebka	شبكة
never	'emmer	عمر
new	zhdïd	جديد
news	khbar	اخبار
newsagency	wakalat lkhbar	وكالة الاخبار
newspaper	zharïda	جريدة
next	zhay	جاي
next to	hda	حدا
nice	zwïn	زوين
night	lïla	ليلا
no	la	لا
nobody	hetta wahed	حتى واحد
noise	şda'	صداع
noisy	kein şda'	كاين صداع
none	walü	والو
noon	weşt nnhar	وسط النهار
north	shamal	شمال
nose	nïf	نيف
nosey	fḍulï	فضولي
not	mashï	ماشي
not yet	mazal	مازال
notebook	karnï	كرني
nothing	walü	والو
novel (book)	qeşşa	قصة
now	daba	دبا
number	raqem	رقم
nurse	fermlïya	فرمليا

O

obvious	bayn	باين
ocean	bhar	بحر
of	dyal	ديال
offence	mukhalafa	مخالفة
office	mektab	مكتب
often	bezzaf	بزاف

oil	zït	زيت
OK	wakha	واخ
old	qdïm	قديم
old city	mdïna qdïma	مدينة قديمة
olive	zïtün	زيتون
olive oil	zït l'üd	زيت زيتون
on	'la	علي
on time	felweqt	في الوقت
once	merra	مرة
one-way (ticket)	mshï	مشي
only	ghïr	غير
open (adj)	mehlül	محلول
to open	hell	حل
operation (surgery)	'amalïya	عملية
operator	teqnï	تقني
opinion	fikra	فكرة
opposite	'eks	عكس
or	'ülla	الا
oral	belheḍra	بالهضرة
orange	lïmün	ليمون
orange (colour)	lïmünï	ليموني
orchestra	ürkestra	اركسترا
order	ṭālāb	طلب
to order	ṭleb	طلب
ordinary	'adï	عادي
organise	neḍḍem	نظم
original	'eşlï	اصلي
other	akhür	اخر
outside	berra	برا
over	füq men	فوق من
overcoat	muntu	منطو
owe	tsal	تسال
owner	mul	مول
oxygen	hwa	هوا

P

pacifier (dummy)	skata	سقتة
package	bakïya	بكية
padlock	qfel	قفل
page	şefha	صفحة

English	Transliteration	Arabic
pain	luzheᶜ	لوجع
painful	kayder	كيضر
paint	ṣbagha	صباغة
to paint	ṣbegh	صبغ
paint (pictures)	rsem	رسم
painter	ṣebbagh	صباغ
paintings	teṣawer	تصور
pair (a couple)	ferda	فردة
palace	qṣer	قصر
pan	meqla	مقلة
pants	serwal	سروال
paper	werqa	ورقة
paper (wrapping)	kaghiṭ	كاغيط
parcel	kūliya	كلية
parents	walidīn	والدين
park	ṣaha	ساحة
to park	wqef	وقف
part	ṭerf	طرف
party (fiesta)	hefla	حفلة
party (politics)	hizab	حزب
passenger	muṣafir	مسافر
passport	pasbōr	باسبور
passport number	nemra dyal lpasbōr	نمرة ديال الباسبور
past	māḍei	ماضي
path	ṭriq ṣghīr	طريق صغير
patient (adj)	ṣebbar	صبار
to pay	khelleṣ	خلص
payment	khlaṣ	خلاص
peace	salam	سلام
peak	raṣ	راس
pedestrian	balīd	بليد
pen	stīlū	ستيلو
penalty	khṭeiya	خطية
pencil	qalam	قلم
penknife	mūs	موس
people	nas	ناس
pepper	lebzār	لبزار
percent	felmya	فالمية
performance	dawer	دور
perfume	rīha	ريحة
permanent	dīma	ديما
permission	rūkhsa	رخصة
personal	shekhṣī	شخصي

personality	shekhṣīya	شخصية
perspire	ᶜreq	عرق
petition	lmūzheb	لموجب
petrol	lișanș	لسانس
pharmacy	farmasyan	فرمسيان
phone book	ktab dyal tīlīfōn	كتاب ديال التليفون
phone box	dalīl dyal tīlīfōn	تليفو ن عمومي
photo	teṣwira	تصويرة
photographer	muṣawwer	مصور
photography	tṣwir	تصوير
to pick up	hezz	هز
picture	teṣwira	تصويرة
piece	ṭerf	طرف
pig	hellūf	حللوف
pill	fanīda	فنيدة
pillow	mkhedda	مخدة
pillowcase	ghesha dyal lmkhedda	غسنا ديال المخدة
pink	fanīdī	فنيدي
pipe	tīyyū	تيبو
pitcher	ghurraf	غراف
place	blāṣa	بلاصة
plain	ᶜadī	عادي
plane	ṭiyyara	طيارة
planet	kewkeb	كوكب
plant	ghers	غرس
to plant	ghers	غرس
plastic	mīkka	ميكة
plate	ṭebṣīl	طبسيل
play (theatre)	temtīl	تمتيل
to play	lᶜeb	لعب
player (sports)	laᶜb	لعاب
playing cards	karta	الكارطة
please	ᶜafak	عفاك
plug (bath)	gfala	قفلة
plug (electricity)	priz	بريز
pocket	zhīb	جيب
poetry	shiᶜr	شعر
poison	semm	سم
police	būlis	بوليس
policeman	būlisī	بوليسي

police station	kumisariya	كميسارية
politician	sīyasī	سياسي
politics	sīyasīya	سياسة
pollution	talawuth	تلوث
pool (swimming)	pīsīn	بيسين
poor	meskīn	مسكين
popular	m'rūf	معروف
port	mersa	مرسي
possible	yemken	يمكن
post code	ramz lbaredī	الرمز البريدي
post office	busṭa	بوسطة
postage	irsal	ارسال
postcard	kart pustal	كارط بوستال
pot	ṭenzhra	طنجرة
potato	bṭāṭā	بطاطا
pottery	fekhkhar	فخار
poverty	faqer	فقير
power	sulṭṭa	سلطة
prayer	muṣllī	مصلي
to prefer	fḍel	فضل
pregnant	hamla	حاملة
to prepare	wzhzhed	وجد
prescription	werqa dyal ṭṭōbīb	ورقة ديال الطبيب
present (gift)	hdīya	هدية
present (time)	daba	داب
presentation	teqdīm	تقديم
president	ra'īs	رئيس
pressure	ḍeghṭ	ضغط
pretty	zwīn	زوين
prevent	mne'	منع
price	taman	تمن
pride	iftīkhar	افتخار
prime minister	wazīr luwwel	وزير الاول
prison	hebs	حبس
prisoner	hebbas	حباس
private	khaṣ	خاص
problem	mūshkīl	مشكل
profession	mihna	مهنة
profit	rbih	ربح
program	bernamezh	برنامج

promise	wa'd	وعد
pronunciation	nuṭq	نطق
proposal	iqtirah	اقتراح
to protect	hfeḍ	حفض
to protest	'areḍ	عارض
to pull	zhbed	جبد
pump	bumba	بومبة
puncture	teqba	تقبة
to punish	'qeb	عقب
puppy	klīyeb	كليب
pure	ṣāfī	صافي
purse	sak	ساك
to push	dfe'	دفع
to put	heṭṭ	حط

Q

quality	zhūda	جودة
quantity	'adad	عدد
to quarrel	dabez	دابز
queen	malīka	ملكة
question	sū'al	سوءال
to question	sewwel	سول
quick	zerba	زربة
quickly	dghīya	دغية
quiet	mhedden	مهدن
to quit	wqef	وقف

R

rabbit	qniya	قنية
racism	'unṣurīya	عنصرية
racquet	rakīta	ركيتة
radiator	radyatur	رديادور
radio	rādyū	راديو
railway station	mheṭṭa dyal tran	محطة ديال التران
rain	shta	شتا
rare	qlīlia	قليلة
rash	hbūb	حبوب
rat	ṭōbba	طوبة
raw	khḍer	خضر
razor	zezwar	زيزوار
razor blades	rizwan	رزوان

English	Translit	Arabic
to read	qra	قراء
ready	mūzhūd	موجود
reason	sabab	سبب
receipt	faktūra	فكتورة
receive	tweşşel	توصل
recent	zhdīd	جديد
recognise	'ref	عرف
recommend	nşeh	نصح
recording	tszhīl	تسجيل
recycling	tzhdīd	تجديد
red	hmer	حمر
referee	hakam	حكم
reference	dalīl	دليل
refrigerator	tellazha	تلاجة
to refund	'uwwed	عوض
to refuse	rfeḍ	رفض
region	nahīya	ناحية
to regret	ndem	ندم
relationship	'alaqa	علاقة
relax	starah	ستارح
religion	dīn	دين
religious	dīnī	ديني
remember	'qel 'la	عقل علي
remote	mun'azil	منعزل
to rent	kra	كراء
to repair	şlah	صلح
to repeat	awed	عاود
ruins	atar	اتار
rules	qawanīn	قوانين
to run	zhra	جرا

S

English	Translit	Arabic
sad	mqelleq	مقلق
safe (adj)	salma	سالمة
safe (n)	khzana	خزانة
salad	shlada	شلادة
salary	'uzhra	اجرة
salt	melha	ملح
same	bhal bhal	بحال بحال
sand	remla	رملة
sandal	sandala	صندلة
sandwich	kaskrūt	كاسكروت

English	Translit	Arabic
sanitary napkins	fōṭa dyal lhīd	فوطة ديال الحيض
Saturday	ssebt	سبت
sausage	sūsīs	سوسيس
save	sellek	سلك
say	gal	قال
to scale	tle'	طلع
scared	khayf	خايف
scenery	menḍer	منظر
school	medrāsa	مدرسة
science	'ulum	علوم
scientist	'ilmī	عالم
scissors	meqqes	مقص
to score	hsab	حساب
screw	vīs	فيس
screwdriver	tūrnūvīs	طرنفيس
sea	bher	بحر
seasick	ddūkha dyal lbher	دوخة ديال البحر
seaside	shaṭī	شطي
seat	kursī	كرسي
seatbelt	şemṭaī	صمطة
second	tanī	تاني
second (time)	tanīya	تانية
secretary	sukritīra	سكرتيرة
see	shaf	شاف
self-service	tserbī raşek	تسربي راسك
sell	ba'	باع
send	şeifeṭ	سفط
sensible	m'qōl	معقول
sentence (words)	zhūmla	جملة
sentence (prison)	thkīm	تحكم
to separate	ferreQ	فرق
series	halaqat	حلقات
service	serbīs	سربيس
sew	kheyyeṭ	خيط
shade	ḍell	ضل
shampoo	shampwan	شامبوان
shape	fōrma	فورمة
share (with)	ferreq	فرق
shave to	hessen	حسن
she	hiya	هي

S

sheep	hawlī	حاولي
sheet (bed)	īzar	ليزار
sheet (of paper)	werqa	ورقة
shelves	mrafeᶜ	مرافع
ship	babūr	بابور
to ship	Sīfṭ ᶜala lbaḥr	صفت علي البحر
shirt	qamīzha	قاميصة
shoe lace	sīr	سير
shoe shop	ḥanūt dyal ṣṣebbaṭ	حانوت ديال صباط
shoes	ṣebbaṭ	صباط
shop	ḥanūt	حانوت
to shop	tqeḍḍa	تقد
short	qṣeir	قصير
shortage	naqs	نقص
shorts	shōrt	شورت
shoulder	ktef	كتاف
to shout	ghowwet	غوت
to show	werra	وري
shower	dūsh	دوش
shrine	muqeddes	مقدس
shut (adj)	msdūd	مسدود
to shut	sedd	سد
shy	heshman	حشمان
sick	mrīḍ	مريض
sickness	merḍa	مرض
side	zhenb	جنب
signature	tawqīᶜ	توقيع
silver	neqra	نكر
similar	bḥal bḥal	بحال بحال
simple	ᶜadī	عادي
sing	ghenna	غني
singer	mughannī	مغني
single (person)	ᶜazrī	عزري
single room	bīt dyal waḥed	بيت ديال واحد
sister	khet	اخت
to sit	gles	كلس
Sit down! gles!		كلس
size	qyas	قياس
to ski	tzhleq	تزلق

skin	zheld	جلد
sky	sma	سماء
sleep	nᶜsa	نعس
sleepy	fīh nnᶜas	فيه النعاس
Slow down! beshwīya ᶜlīk!		بشوي عليك
slow	beshwīya	بشوي
slowly	beshwīya	بشوي
small	ṣghir	صغير
smell	rīha	ريحة
to smell	shemm	شم
to smile	tbessem	تبسم
smoke (n)	dukhkhan	دخان
smoke a cigarette	kma	كما
snake	hensh	حنش
snow	telzh	تلج
soap	ṣābūn	صابون
soccer	kōra	كرة
socks	tqasher	تقاشر
soft	rṭeb	رطب
soft drink	munāḍa	موناضة
solid	qaṣeh	قاصح
some	shī	شي
somebody	shī waḥed	شي واحد
something	shī hzha	شي حاجة
sometimes	bāᶜdlmerrat	بعض المرات
son	weld	ولد
song	aghniyya	اغنية
soon	deghīya	دغيا
sound	ṣōt	صوت
sour (unseasoned)	mssūs	مسوس
south	zhanūb	جنوب
space	tīsaᶜ	تيساع
speak	tkellem	تكلم
special	khaṣṣ	خاص
specialist	mukhtaṣ	مختص
speed	surᶜa	سرعة
speed limit	hedd ssurᶜa	حد السرعة
spend the night	bat	بات
spicy (hot)	har	حار
spoon	mᶜelqa	معلقة
sport	rīyaḍa	رياضة

D I C T I O N A R Y

sprain	fdeᶜ	فدع
spring (season)	rbiᶜ	ربيع
square (in town)	saha	ساحة
stadium	tiran	تيران
stairs	drūzh	دروج
stale	qdīm	قديم
stamp	tanber	تنبر
standard (usual)	'adī	عادي
star	nezhma	نجمة
to start	bda	بدأ
station	mheṭṭa	محطة
stay	bqa	بقي
to steal	sreq	سرق
steam	bukhar	بخار
steep	waqef	واقف
stomach	kersh	كرش
stone	hezhra	حجرة
stop light	ḍu lhmer	ضو الاحمر
stop sign	sṭup	سطوب
Stop! weqef!		وقف!
storm	ᶜaṣifa	عاصفة
story	qeṣṣa	قصة
stove	furnu	فورنو
straight	nīshan	نيشان
strange	fshishkel	فشي شكل
stranger	ghrib	غريب
stream	wad	واد
street	zenqa	زنقة
strength	qowwa	قوة
strike	iḍrab	اضراب
string	kheyyet	خيط
to stroll	tsara	تصرة
strong	shīh	شيح
stubborn	rasu qaseh	راسه كاسح
student	ṭālib	طالب
stupid	mkellekh	مكلخ
suburb	hay	حي
success	nazhah	نجاح
suffer	tᶜaddeb	تعذب
sugar	sūkkar	سكر
suitcase	balīza	بليزة
summer	ssīf	صيف

sun	shems	شمس
sunglasses	nḍaḍer dyal shshems	نضاضر ديال شمس
sunny	mshemes	مشمس
sunrise	shruq dyal shshems	شروق ديال الشمس
sunset	ghrub dyal shshems	شروق ديال الشمس
sure	m'ekked	ماكد
surface mail	bared ᶜadī	بريد عادي
surprise	ᶜla ghifla	تلي غفلة
sweater	trīkū	تريكو
sweet	hlew	حلو
sweets	helwat	حلوة
to swim	ᶜūm	عوم
swimming	ᶜuman	عومان
swimming pool	pīsīn	بيسين
swimsuit	hwayezh dyal lᶜuman	حوايج ديال العومان
sword	sif	سيف
syringe	ībra	ابرة

T

English	Transliteration	Arabic
T-shirt	tī shūrt	تي شرت
table	ṭābla	طابلة
tablet (medicine)	fanīda	فنيدة
tail	qezzība	قزيبة
tailor	kheyyaṭ	خياط
take (away)	dda	دي
to talk	tkellem	تكلم
tall	ṭwīl	طويل
tampons	zīf dyal ddemm	زيف ديال الدم
tape	skātsh	سكوتش
to taste	daq	داق
tasty	bnīna	بنينة
tax	ḍārība	ضريبة
taxi	tāksī	تكسي
taxi stand	blaṣa dyal taksī	بلاصة ديال التاكسي
tea	atei	اتاي
teacher	'ūstad	استاذ

English	Transliteration	Arabic
teaching	t'līm	تعليم
team	ferqa	فرقة
tear (crying)	dem'a	دمعة
teeth	snan	سنان
telegram	tīligram	تليكرام
telephone	telefun	تليفون
television	telfaza	تلفزة
to tell	gal	كال
temperature (fever)	skhana	سخانة
tennis	tīnīs	تنيس
tennis court	tīran dyal ttīnīs	تيران ديال التنيس
tent	gītūn	كيطون
tenth	'asher	عاشر
terrible	khayb	خايب
test	imtīhan	امتحان
thank	shker	شكر
Thank you. shukran		شكرا
theatre	mesreh	مسرح
they	huma	هما
thick	ghlīḍ	غليظ
thief	sheffer	شفار
thin	rqeiq	رقيق
thing	hazha	حاجة
think	fker	فكر
third	tulut	تولوت
thirst	'tesh	عطش
thirsty	'aṭshan	عطشان
this (one)	hada	هدا
thought	tefkīr	تفكير
thread	kheyṭ	خيط
throat	helq	حلق
throw	lah	لاح
ticket	werqa	ورقة
tight	mzeyyer	مزير
time	weqt	وقت
tin (can)	huk	حق
tin opener	ssarūt	ساروت
tip (gratuity)	tedwira	تضويرة

tired	'eyyan	عيان
tobacco	taba	طابة
tobacco kiosk	ṣaka	صاكة
today	lyūm	اليوم
together	mezhmu'in	مجموعين
toilet	bīt lma	بيت الماء
toilet paper	kaghiṭ dyal bit lma	كاغيط ديال بيت الماء
tomorrow	ghedda	غدا
tongue	lsan	لسان
tonight	had llīla	هد الليلة
too (also)	hetta	حتي
too much	bezzaf	بزاف
tooth	senna	سنة
toothache	ṣḍa' dyal ssnan	صداع ديال السنان
toothbrush	shīṭa d ssnan	شيطة ده سنان
toothpaste	m'zhūn dyal ssnan	معجون ديال السنان
top	qīmma	قمة
torch	ppīl	بيل
to touch	qāṣ	قاس
tour	tzhwīsa	طجويصة
tourist	sa'ih	سايح
towel	fuṭa	فوطة
tower	ṣem'ā	سمعة
town	mdīna	مدينة
to trade	tbadel	تبادل
traffic	zнam	زحام
train	tran	تران
train station	mhetta dyal tran	محطة ديال التران
translate	terzhem	ترجم
translation	terzhama	ترجمة
travel	ṣāfer	سافر
travel agency	mekteb 'asfar	مكتب السفر
travellers cheque	shek sīyahī	شيك سياحي
tree	shezhra	شجرة
trip	ṣefra	سفرة

trousers	serwel	سروال
truck	kamiyū	كاميو
true	haqiqi	حقيقي
trust	tiqa	ثقة
truth	huqq	حق
try	hawel	حاول
turn (n)	nūba	نوبة
Turn left.		
ḍōr 'l līser		دور علي اليسار
Turn right.		
ḍōr 'l līmen		دور علي اليمين
Turn!		
ḍur!		دور !
TV	telfaza	تلفزة
twice	zhuzh khṭrat	جوج خطرات
twins	twam	توام
to type	ḍreb 'al daktīlū	ضرب علي الدكتيلو
tyres	bnuwat	بنوات

U

umbrella	mḍell	مضل
under	teht men	تحت من
understand	fhem	فهم
understood	mefhūm	مفهوم
unemployed	shumur	شمور
unemployment	shumazh	شماج
unions	itīhad	اتحاد
universe	kawn	كون
university	zhamī'a	جامعة
unsafe	khaṭar	خطر
untie	hell	حل
until	hetta	حتي
unusual	'zhīb	عجيب
up	fuq	فوق
uphill	tale'	طالع
upset (mad)	mqelleq	مقلق
urgent	mezrub	مزروب
to use	ste'mel	ستعمل
useful	ṣalha	صالحة

vacant	khawī	خاوي
vacation	'utla	عطلة
vaccination	zhelba	جلبة
valley	wad	واد
valuable	ghalī	غالي
value (price)	qīma	قيمة
vase	mehbeq	محبق
vegetables	khḍra	خضرة
vegetarian	makayakūlsh lhem	مكا يكلش اللحم
vegetation	khuḍra	خضرة
vein	'erq	عرق
very	bezzaf	بزاف
video cassette	kassīt vidyu	كاسيط فيديو
view	menḍer	منضر
village	qerya	قرية
vine	'enba	عنبة
virus	zhartūma	جرثومة
visa	t'shīra	تاشيرة
to visit	zar	زار
vitamin	vītamīn	فيتامين
voice	ṣuṭ	صوت
to vomit	tqeyya	تقية
to vote	ṣowweṭ	صويت

W

to wait	tsenna	تسني
waiter	garsun	كارسون
to wake up	faq	فاق
to walk	temsha 'la rezhlīn	تمشي علي الرجلين
wall	heyṭ	حيط
to want	bgha	بغي
war	harb	حرب
warm	dafi	دافي
warn	nebbeh	نبه
wash	ghsel	غسل
wash (clothes)	ṣebben	صبن

English	Transliteration	Arabic
washing machine	makīna dyal ghsīl	مكينة ديال الغسيل
to watch	shaf	شاف
watch	magana	مكنة
Watch out!	ᶜndak!	عندك!
water	lma	الماء
waterfall	shllalat	شلالات
watermelon	dellah	دلاح
wave (ocean)	mūzha	موجة
way	ṭrīq	طريق
we	hna	حنا
weak	dᶜīf	ضعيف
wealthy	ghanī	غني
to wear	lbes	لبس
weather	hal	حال
wedding	ᶜers	عرس
week	ssīmana	صيمنة
weekend	lkhīr dyal sīmana	اخردیال الصیمنة
weigh	ᶜber	عبير
weight	ᶜbar	عبار
welcome	mrehba	مرحبا
well	bīr	بير
west	gherb	غرب
wet	fazeg	فازݣ
What?	ashnū?	اشنو؟
wheel	rweiḍa	رويضة
wheelchair	kursī mutaharrik	كرسي متحرك
When?	īmta?	امتي
Where?	fīn?	فين
Which?	ashmen?	اشمن ؟
white	byeḍ	بيض
Who?	shkūn?	شكون ؟

whole	kamel	كامل
Why? ᶜlash?		علاش ؟
wide	waseᶜ	واسع
wife	mra	مراة
wild animal	hayawan mutawahhesh	حيوومتوحش
to win	rbeh	ربح
wind	rīh	ربح
window	sherzhem	شرجم
wine	shrab	شراب
wings	zhnah	جناح
winner	rabeh	رابح
winter	shta	شتا
wire	selk dyal ḍō	سلك ديال الضو
wise	meᶜqōl	معقول
to wish	tmenna	تمني
with	mᶜa	مع
within	dakhel	داخل
within an hour	men daba saᶜa	من داب ساعة
without	bla	بلا
woman	mra	مرا
wonderful	ʾazhīb	عجيب
wood	ᶜwad	عواد
woods (forest)	ghaba	غابة
wool	ṣuf	صوف
word	kelma	كلمة
to work	khdem	خدم
work	khedma	خدمة
work permit	rōkhṣa dyal khedma	رخصة ديال الخدمة
world	ᶜalam	عالم
worms	dūd	دود
worried	mqelleq	مقلق
worth	qima	قيمة
wound	zherh	جرح
to write	kteb	كتب
writer	katib	كاتب
wrong	ghalaṭ	غلط

X

x-ray	rādyu	رادیو

Y

year	ʿam	عام
yellow	şfer	صفر
yes	īyeh	ايبه
yesterday	lbareh	البارح
yet	mazal	مازال

yogurt	danūn	دانون
you	'nta	انت
young	şghir	صغیر
youth (collective)	shabab	شباب
youth hostel	dar shshabab	دار الشباب

Z

zipper	sensla	سنسلة
zoo	hadīqa	حدیقة دل
	delhayawa	حیوان

INDEX

SUSTAINABLE TRAVEL

As the climate change debate heats up, the matter of sustainability becomes an important part of the travel vernacular. In practical terms, this means assessing our impact on the environment and local cultures and economies – and acting to make that impact as positive as possible. Here are some basic phrases to get you on your way …

COMMUNICATION & CULTURAL DIFFERENCES

I'd like to learn some of your local dialects.
bghīt netʿellem shi
lahazhat dyalkum

بغيت نتعلم شي
لهجات ديالكم

Would you like me to teach you some English?
wash bghitini nʿelmek
shwiya dial nnegliziya?

واش بغيتيني نعلمك
شويا ديال نكليزية؟

Is this a local or national custom?
wash hadi ʿada maHelliya
wella waṭaniya?

واش هادي عادة محلية
ولا وطنية؟

I respect your customs.
taneHtarem lʿadat dyalkum

تنحترم لعادات ديالكم

COMMUNITY BENEFIT & INVOLVEMENT

What sorts of issues is this community facing?
shnu hiya lmashakil
dyal nnas?

شنو هي المشاكل
ديال الناس؟

freedom of the press	Hurriyat eṣṣaHafa	حرية الصحافة
police and army reform	iṣlaH lbulis welʿesker	إصلاح البوليس والعسكر
political unrest	eṭṭerab siyyasi	اضطراب سياسي
religious freedom	Hurriyat eddīn	حرية الدين
rights of women and children	Huquq lmarʾa weṭṭifl	حقوق المرأة والطفل

I'd like to volunteer my skills.
bghīt neṭṭewweʿ
beṣṣenʿa dyali

بغيت نتطوع
بالصنعة ديالي

Are there any volunteer programs available in the area?
wash kayenshi baramizh
dyal lmutaṭawwiʿine
fhad lmazhāl?

واش كاينشي برامج
ديال المتطوعين
فهاد المجال؟

ENVIRONMENT

Does your company have a green policy?
wash ʿend sharika
dyalkum siyasa biʾiya?

واش عند الشركة
ديالكم سياسة بيئية؟

Where can I recycle this?
fin nelqa errusiklazh
dyal had shi?

فين نلقا الروسيكلاج
ديال هاد الشي؟

TRANSPORT

Can we get there by public transport?
wash nqedru nweṣlu
ltemma bṭṭubis?

واش نقدرو نوصلو
لتما بالطوبيس؟

Can we get there by bicycle?
wash nqedru nweṣlu
ltemma belbeshklīt?

واش نقدرو نوصلو
لتما بالبشكليط؟

I'd prefer to walk there.
nfeddel netmeshsha lhih

نفضل نتمشى لهيه

Does your airline have a carbon-offset scheme?
wash ʿend sharika ṭṭayaran
dyalkum bernamazh
ltaʿweeḍ lkarbūn?

واش عند شركة الطيران
ديالكم برنامج
لتعويض الكاربون؟

ACCOMMODATION

I'd like to stay at a locally-run hotel.
bghīt neskun f uṭīl maHelli

بغيت نسكن فأوطيل محلي

Are there any ecolodges here?
    wash kayen shi 'uṭilat
    berra lmdina fṭṭabi°a?

واش كاين شي أوطيلات
برا المدينة فالطبيعة؟

Can I turn the air conditioning off and open the window?
    yemkenliya neṭfi
    leklimatizur wenHel
    shsherzhem?

يمكن لي نطفي
لكليماتيزور ونحل
الشرجم؟

There's no need to change my sheets, they're still clean.
    bla ma yetbeddlu lizur,
    mazalin nqiyyin

بلا ما يتبدلو ليزور,
مازالين نقيين

SHOPPING

Where can I buy locally produced goods/souvenirs?
    fin yemken liya neshri
    ssel°a/li suvunir dyal leblad?

فين يمكن ليا نشري
السلعة/لي سوفونير ديال البلاد؟

Do you sell Fair Trade products?
    wash katbi°u ssel°a
    dyal ttizhara lmunsifa?

واش كاتبيعو السلعة
ديال التجارة المنصفة؟

What's this made from?
    mennash mesnu° hadshi?

مناش مصنوع هاد الشي؟

copper	nHas	النحاس
leather	zheld	الجلد
silver	ennuqra	النقرة

FOOD

Where can I find the health-food section?
    fin nelqa lzhiha dyal
    lmakla ṣṣiHHiya?

فين نلقى الجهة ديال
الماكلا الصحية؟

Can you tell me what traditional foods I should try?
    teqder tgulliya ashmen makla
    teqlidiya njerreb?

تقدر تقول لي آشمن ماكلا
تقليدية نجرب؟

Is this locally produced?
wash hadi sel'a dyal leblad?
واش هادي سلعة ديال البلاد؟

Do you sell organic produce?
wash katbi'u lmuntazhat
l'uḍwiya?
واش كاتبيعو المنتجات
العضوية؟

SIGHTSEEING

Does your company …?	wash shsharika dyalkum …?	واش الشركة ديالكم...؟
donate money to charity	tatberre' belflous elkhayriyya	تاتبرع بالفلوس لخيرية
hire local guides	tatkri lgyad local	تاتكري لكياد لوكال
visit local businesses	tatzur lmaHellat tijariyya lmaHelliya	تاتزور المحلات التجارية المحلية

Are cultural tours available?
wash kayenshi jawlat
thaqafiya?
واش كاينشي جولات
ثقافية؟

I'd like to hire a local guide.
bghīt nakhud gid maHelli
بغيت ناخد كيد محلي

Does the guide speak the local language?
wash lgid tayetkellem
llugha lmaHelliya?
واش الكيد تايتكلم
اللغة المحلية؟

Berber	tamazight	تمازيغت
Tarifit	tarifit	تاريفيت
Tashelhiyt	tashelHit	تاشلحيت

EMERGENCIES

English	Transliteration	Arabic
Help!	ᶜṭeqnī!	عتقني!
Stop!	wqef!	وقف!
Go away!	sīr fhalek!	سير فحالك!
Thief!	sheffar!	شفار!
Fire!	lᶜafiya!	العافية!
Danger!	khatar!	خطر!
Help me please!	ᶜawennī ᶜafak!	عاوني عفاك!
Emergency!	'mestaᶜzhel!	مستعجل!
Call the police!	ᶜayyeṭ ᶜla lbūlīs!	عيط على! البوليس
Call the ambulance!	ᶜayyeṭ ᶜla ssayyara del 'asᶜaf!	عيط على السيارة دال اسعاف!